Bhopal

Bhopal

P.K. De

NIYOGI
BOOKS

Published by

NIYOGI BOOKS

D-78, Okhla Industrial Area, Phase-I
New Delhi-110 020, INDIA
Tel: 91-11-26816301, 49327000
Fax: 91-11-26810483, 26813830
Email: niyogibooks@gmail.com
Website: www.niyogibooksindia.com

Editor: Upama Biswas
Design: Nabanita Das

ISBN: 978-93-83098-81-1
Publication: 2015

Printed at: Niyogi Offset Pvt. Ltd., New Delhi, India

In fond memory
of my parents

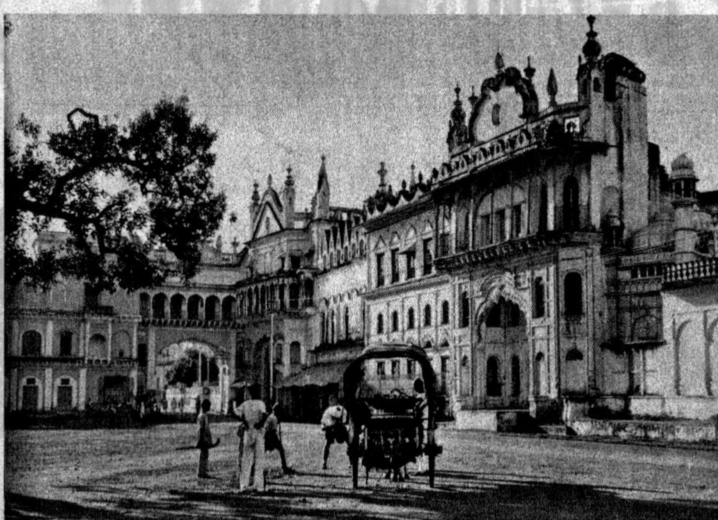

Saukat Mahal, Bhopal

Contents

Preface

In British India, the Muslim-ruled kingdom of Bhopal was the largest princely state next only to the Nizam's Hyderabad. Like any other principality of India, Bhopal too has its many-splendoured history. The story of how Bhoj-pal, the tiny, ancient, non-descript village of Malwa, grew within a span of thousand years into a large kingdom called Bhopal and then progressed further to win the crown of a modern state capital is quite absorbing. The old city of today's Bhopal, better known as Begums' Bhopal, retains certain quaint picturesque charm with a rustic halo around. It may be said that Begums' Bhopal is a conundrum; it can be categorised neither as a city nor as an urbanised rural habitation. New Bhopal on the other hand, is a posh, upcoming metropolis with all the paraphernalia of modern living. But all inclusive, the capital city known today as Bhopal, together with its territorial ambit, occupies an exceptional place in the country. This strange uniqueness of Bhopal has been unveiled in the present text for the avid readers and travel enthusiasts to assess, admire and enjoy. The narrative keeps the reader engrossed all the while with numerous interesting legends, myths and strange beliefs, many of which trace its roots to antiquity. The pleasure is endless as we go through the narrative detailing from the pre-historic antiquities of a place to the over-two-century-long hierarchy founded by a Pathan warlord in India, which happens to be contemporary to the existence and growth of present-day metropolitan cities like Chennai and Kolkata.

Journey through the annals of history

Located centrally in the Indian subcontinent and encircled by several other states, Madhya Pradesh is aptly called the heartland of the country. In fact, during the British regime the state was known as the Central Province with Jabalpur as its capital. After reorganisation of the states of the Indian Republic in 1956, to which the former princely state of Bhopal had been merged, a new state of Madhya Pradesh was formed with the city of Bhopal as its capital. Sprawling widely on the forested southern slope of the great Vindhya Range, Bhopal with its beautiful lakes, undulating terrains with charming greenery, hilly landscape and above all—an interesting rustic appeal occupies a unique position amongst many other prominent cities of the country. Bhopal, for several reasons, may be considered very special when judged in the perspective of its antiquity as well as its kaleidoscopic history.

Geologically, about 65 million years ago the Indian peninsula was formed as a disintegrated fragment of the vast supercontinent, Gondwanaland. Major parts of south and central India originated as extensive upland of volcanic origin known as the Deccan Traps. Much later, about 1,00,000 years ago from the present times, the Deccan Traps for the first time witnessed the emergence of primitive human beings. For over a long period, the Southern Plateau and the

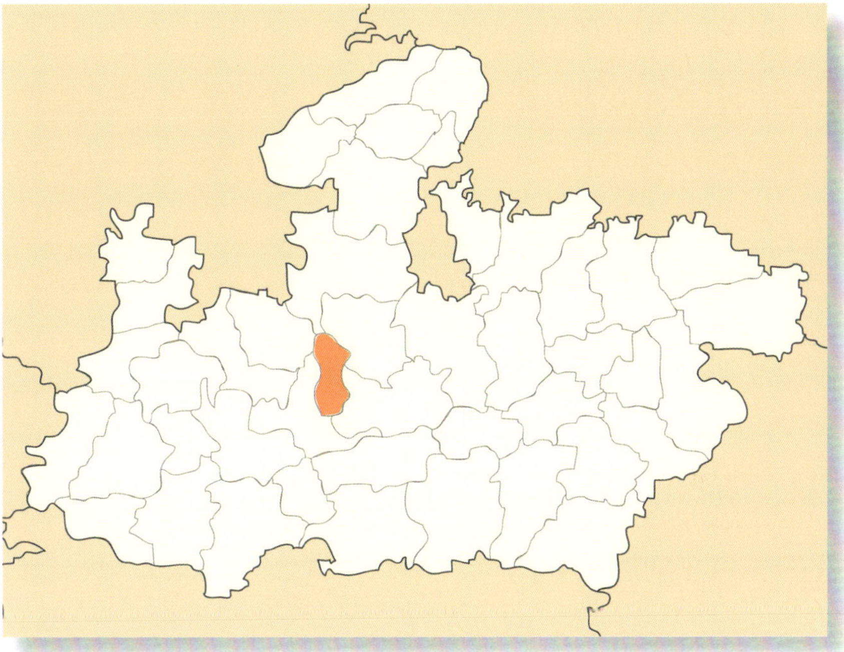

Bhopal, centrally located in Madhya Pradesh

Vindhya Range continued to remain as the habitat of the Paleolithic, then Mesolithic, and later of the Neolithic men living in cave shelters. Many such rock dwellings of the pre-historic man have been discovered in the vicinity of Bhopal, establishing the historical roots of the region. Gradually with the passage of time, this part of central India, known in history as Malwa Plateau, had seen the advent of civilisation, inhabited and ruled by the aboriginal tribes. After still many long years, there appeared some comparatively sophisticated intruders from the North—the Aryans. They came in large groups at different phases of the development of civilisation, established several kingdoms and dynasties, such as the kingdoms of Avanti and Satavahana, the dynasties of the Mauryas, the Guptas, the Paramaras and many others. Thereafter, during the medieval period came the Pathans, Mughals and finally came the British from across the seas.

Early History

From the mid-10th century Malwa remained under the control of the Paramaras who established their capital at Dhar. Paramara king Bhojadeva or Raja Bhoj ruled Malwa from AD 1010 till 1063. Some historians believing in analogy would identify the name of Raja Bhoj with Emperor Vikramaditya, the hero of the story on the enchanted throne of the latter as has been narrated in the famous Sanskrit text "Vikrama Charitra".

Raja Bhoj, from whom Bhopal derives its name (Bhoj + Pal = Bhopal), was a philosopher, king and a polymath of medieval India. The word Bhoja means "beautiful" and appears to be the name of the tribe—the descendants of Mahabhoja mentioned in the Mahabharata. Raja Bhoj was a great warrior who had successfully resisted all the Islamic invasions of India during his lifetime. He was a great scholar too and wrote 84 books on varied subjects, of which several still survive. His extensive writings covered multifaceted fields—philosophy, poetry, medicine, veterinary science, phonetics, yoga and archery. Under his rule the kingdom of Malwa and its capital Dhar became one of the principal intellectual centres of India. Raja Bhoj, being a religious person, constructed numerous temples in his kingdom; of these the gigantic shrine of Bhojeshwara Shiva in Bhojpur near Bhopal is worth a mention for housing the world's largest Shiva Lingam. Built on the bank of river Betwa the temple is an architectural marvel. The learned king also established the Bhojshala—a centre for Sanskrit studies, and also built a temple dedicated to Goddess Saraswati in Dhar, his capital. However, the most significant of his constructive works was in the field of water conservation and irrigation. At Bhojpur, his second citadel, he created a grand extensive lake called Sagar Tal by harnessing the waters of river Betwa which was held alongside a massive dam. Lake and the dam both inclusive, it was the largest man-made water reservoir in Asia covering an area of 400 sq. km; the vast sheet of water not only catered to the irrigational needs for a large part of his kingdom but also helped nurture biodiversity. Several other smaller lakes in and around present-day Bhopal are also the contributions of Raja Bhoj. Recently, a 32-foot high standing figure of the Raja has been erected within the Bada Talab (Upper Lake) of the city as a fond commemoration.

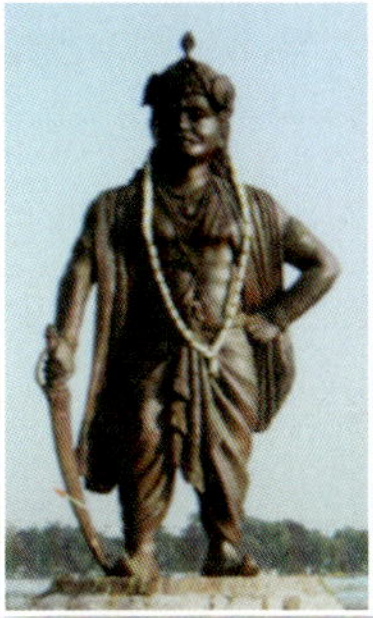
Statue of Raja Bhoj on Upper Lake

After the Raja's death in AD 1063, his successors ruled Malwa until about 1305 when the Pathan sultanate of Delhi conquered the kingdom. Later, the invasion of Taimur in 1398 devastated Delhi and the sultanate became fragmented into several independent small kingdoms. Delhi's Mughal governor in Malwa, Dilwar Khan, too declared himself as an independent sultan and established his capital at Mandu. After his demise, his son Hoshang Shah succeeded and ruled Malwa from AD 1405 till 1435. As the legend goes, during his rule some local wealthy merchants complained that their trade caravans were being looted regularly by bandits who had taken shelter under the enormous dam of the Sagar Tal. Hoshang Shah, in an attempt to capture the eluding looters, ordered the destruction of their hideout, the great dam that had been standing there for over four centuries bestowing enormous benefits to the land and the people. As per history, the execution of his order to demolish the ancient colossus dam required the services of 400 men over a period of almost three months. Also, it had taken several years for all the water to flow out; later, on the dry bed of the lake came up nearly three hundred villages. After the extinction of Sagar Tal, the refreshing, cool climate of the entire region had given way to long spells of dry and warm weather persisting almost the year round.

Medieval Period

The Pathan sultans of Malwa were ultimately defeated by the mighty Gonds, who were rather sophisticated descendants of the local aborigines. Establishing several small kingdoms all over Malwa region they ruled till the early 18th century when Bhopal was a non-descript tiny village in the Gond country. The fortified city of Bhopal was founded afterwards by a valiant Pathan soldier named Dost Mohammad Khan who fled from his native village Tirah, on the border of modern-day Pakistan and Afghanistan, having committed some heinous crime in his homeland. In the late 17th century this young ambitious Pathan (Afghan) warrior crossed into India on horse-back and reached Jalalabad all alone. His dream was to join the Mughal Emperor Aurangzeb's army as a soldier with the hope of seeking his fortune in a foreign land. He was taken in by Mir Fazlullah—the custodian of arms in Aurangzeb's forces. A fierce and valiant fighter, Dost Mohammad had displayed outstanding valour and cunning in many battles and rose steadily through the ranks. Around 1704 he was given the charge of quelling the rebellion in Bundelkhand, led by Kashko Khan. In a fierce battle Dost eliminated Kashko and the rebellion was crushed. As a reward he was given the charge of Malwa region. After the death of

Aurangzeb in 1707, as the Mughal Empire was falling apart, Dost left the Mughals and became a mercenary. With his troops he started providing military services for money to local chieftains in the politically unstable region of Malwa. In 1709 he took on lease the Gond pargana of Berasia close to the village of Bhopal. Thereafter he married a Rajput princess of the royal family of Mangalgarh state nearby. After the death of the issueless dowager queen of Mangalgarh, Dost usurped her domain too. Later, he also annexed several other adjacent territories and after settling himself well in the sizable kingdom thus acquired, he established his own citadel at Jagdishpur near Bhopal renaming it as Islamnagar.

In the meantime, Bhopal and its surrounding region had become a part of the Gond kingdom ruled by Nizam Shah, a tribal warlord. Bhopal had, by then, developed into a prosperous village with some fortifications around. Nizam Shah also built a charming seven-storey palace that would overlook both the Upper and Lower Lakes, for his beautiful wife, Rani Kamlapati. Interesting Gond legends narrate how on moonlit nights the Rani would emerge out of her water-side palatial abode to enjoy the pleasure of drifting across the cool tranquil water in her barge that was shaped like a blooming lotus, while a train of 500 maids would follow her rowing in boats. As ill luck would have it, over an old enmity the king Nizam Shah was poisoned and killed by his nephew and rival Alam Shah, also a Gond, king of Chainpur-Bari. Vulnerable, insecure and seething with anger to avenge her husband's death the Rani approached the mercenary Dost Mohammad and promised him a large sum of money for the head of the killer. Some versions of history state that the Rani had tied a rakhi acknowledging the services of Dost as a brother, who had dutifully fulfilled her wishes. Although immensely grateful the

Rani could not pay the promised sum to Dost. Instead she managed to give him half the sum and gifted the village of Bhopal to him. Again, according to some version of history it is said that Dost was so enamoured by the beauty of the Rani that he sent the widowed Rani Kamlapati a marriage proposal which she hatefully refused; feeling quite insulted and greatly upset, she committed suicide by drowning in the Upper Lake. Another version says that on her refusal the angry Dost decided to marry her forcibly and so he started killing the Rani's trusted aides on whom she depended for safety. Feeling helpless and insecure Rani Kamlapati had committed suicide along with some of her maids. However, it remains a fact that after the Rani's death her young son Nawal Shah who inherited her estate was treacherously killed by the ambitious Dost Mohammad, who then seized control of the Rani's kingdom.

In 1722 Dost transformed the village of Bhopal into a well-fortified city naming it Fatehgarh after his Rajput wife Fateh Bibi and himself assumed the title "Nawab" of the kingdom of Bhopal. To consolidate his position further in the royal Mughal court of Delhi, Dost developed intimacy with the Sayyid brothers, his Afghan kinsmen; these two brothers in the Mughal court were highly influential and were acclaimed as king-makers. Dost gratified the two Sayyids in various ways so that they should fetch for him Delhi's "sanad" recognising his independent status of regency. But such underhand tricky manoeuvres enraged the powerful nobleman Nizam-ul-Mulk of Hyderabad. As Aurangzeb's great general and the governor of the South, the Nizam exercised political control over central India as a whole. His forces invaded Bhopal and the hapless Dost Mohammad had to settle for peace surrendering a large chunk of his territory as the price.

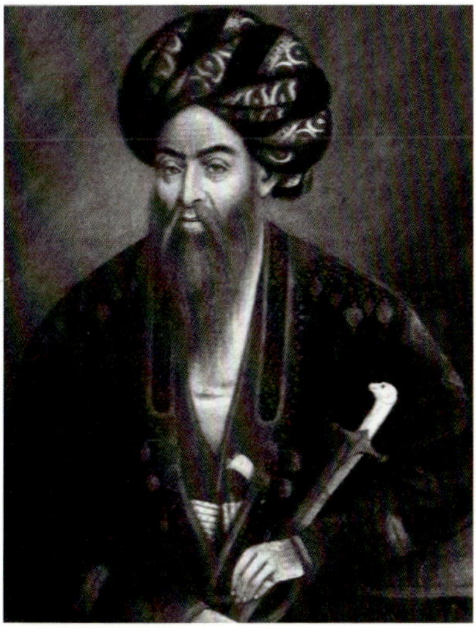

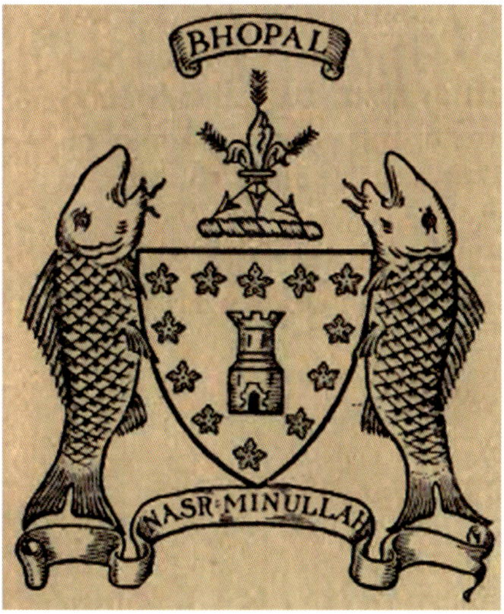

Left: Dost Mohammad Khan, founder of the Pathan dynasty of Bhopal
Right: Coat of arms, Bhopal

In around 1723, Dost went on a pilgrimage to Ajmer Sharif for paying homage at the dargah of the revered Sufi saint Khwaja Moinuddin Chisti. Displaying a great show of respect he sought blessings of the saint at the sacred mazar (shrine), since it was just after his assuming the title of "Nawab". The devout followers of the cult of Sufism known as Chistiyas, who were attending the holy shrine, felt highly impressed on seeing his piety as well as his ardent devotion and readily accepted his warm invitation of going to Bhopal and settling in his capital for promoting and spreading the message of mystic Sufism amongst the masses.

Some of the Chistiyas did come to Bhopal but they preferred to be sheltered atop a hill in the area of Bairagarh close by, rather than staying in the crowded capital. A dargah of the Sufis still exists near the Raja Bhoj Airport even to this day. However, the mystics had shifted once again to a place called Tila Jamalpura where a 300-year-old tradition of Sufi fusion music is still alive. Here several assorted groups of the Chistiya order and their devout Hindu neighbours gather every Thursday for musical recitals; they display to the world outside how best the Quranic renditions and Vedic chants blend together. Even though, radically different in style and presentation, this mixed musical soiree creates a tranquil atmosphere of harmony and peace.

It is believed that Dost Mohammad Khan's wife, a religious Rajput princess who was respected by the Hindus and Muslims alike, played the most important role in spreading the culture of Sufism and religious integration that got deeply ingrained in the psyche of all the Bhopalites irrespective of individual religious affiliations. Perhaps this rare psychic influence together with several other factors had so far enabled the people of Bhopal to maintain a spirit of communal harmony. That the days of Sufi mysticism are not yet over is evident from the recent International Conference on Sufism held in Bhopal on November 2011; where all the assembled delegates planned to establish an international university of Sufism in the near future, hoping that the institution would build a spiritual bridge of religious understanding between the East and the West.

After the death of Dost Mohammad in 1728, his descendants, about 12 of them in succession, became the all-powerful nawabs of the kingdom. For 226 years they ruled the state until it ultimately merged with the Union Republic of India in 1949. Thereafter the nawabs were merely titular heads without any real power to rule. The genealogy of the Pathan ruling dynasty is given below:

Nawabs of Bhopal

Nawab Dost Mohammad Khan
(1723-1728)

Nawab Yar Mohammad Khan
(1728-1742)

Nawab Faiz Mohammad Khan
(1742-1777)

Nawab Hayat Mohammad Khan
(1777-1807)

Nawab Ghous Mohammad Khan
(1807-1826)

Nawab Wazir Mohammad Khan
(in opposition; 1807-1816)

Nawab Nazar Mohammad Khan
(de facto Ruler; 1816-1819)

Nawab Qudsia Begum
(as Regent; 1819-1837)

Nawab Jahangir Mohammad Khan
(1837-1844)

Nawab Qudsia Begum
(as Ruler; 1844-1860)

Nawab Sikandar Jahan Begum
(1860-1868)

Nawab Shah Jahan Begum
(1868-1901)

Nawab Sultan Jahan Begum
(1901-1926)

Nawab Hamidullah Khan
(as Ruler; 1926-1947)
(as titular Nawab; 1949-1960)

Nawab Sultan Sajida Begum
(as titular Nawab; 1960-1995)

Nawab Mansoor Ali Khan Pataudi
(as titular Nawab; 1995-2011)

These nawabs, four of them women, ruled Bhopal for over two centuries; and surprisingly, the state had seen its golden days only during the regency of the four aristocratic ladies who assumed title as "Nawab Begum". They reigned in succession for over 107 years. In fact, the most fascinating part in the history of Bhopal is this century-long tenure of the nawab begums when Bhopal, the second largest Muslim-ruled state after Hyderabad achieved overall progress in various spheres. No wonder then, that the city is fondly regarded as the "Begums' Bhopal". The males in general proved themselves as insignificant figures, rulers of little value. Going by history, they mostly remained occupied either in fighting with the neighbouring states, or with the invading Marathas, or amongst themselves, each claiming their right to the throne. While majority of them would seek an easygoing comfortable life, full of pleasures and entertainments, none could spare time for administering the development and progress of the state. At times there would be even more than one nawab, each in defiance of the other! Compared to their male counterparts the begums were wise, efficient and without any religious bias; they ruled the state confidently and with firm hands. In reality, history has never witnessed such a century-long glorious reign by successive women regents one after the other. Admittedly, the legacy in the royal family had descended consecutively on women because of the absence of male heirs; but the reason behind the administrative acumen of the nawab begums must be attributed to the characteristic dominant force that had been inherent in these aristocratic women who were born to rule.

Nawab Dost Mohammad Khan was succeeded by his son Yar Mohammmed Khan in 1728. In the meantime the powerful

Marathas (during 1730s) had been wresting power in central India. The successors of Dost Mohammad had a tough time dealing with such frequent confrontations. The Marathas conquered several states nearby, including Indore and Gwalior. However, the kingdom of Bhopal somehow managed to continue as a Muslim-ruled, independent state in between these Hindu kingdoms. The Mughal Empire had been crumbling to pieces since the death of Emperor Aurangzeb and the next rulers, his worthless successors, never succeeded in resisting the frequent onslaughts of the plundering Maratha forces. Muhammad Shah, the hapless Mughal ruler sought help from two of his trusted allies—the Nizam-ul-Mulk of Hyderabad and Raja Sawai Jaisingh of Amber. In the battle of 1737 fought near Bhopal, the combined forces of the Mughal and Rajput soldiers led by the Nizam, though overwhelming in number, was totally defeated by the troops of the Maratha Peshwa Balaji Bajirao. As a result, the Mughal Empire became further wrecked while the Nizam lost his control over Bhopal. The independent state of Bhopal was reduced to a mere protectorate of the Marathas to whom the nawabs and the noblemen had to pay regular revenue for maintaining peace as well as political security. The system had continued for another eighty years until the British under the East India Company made their appearance in the scene.

Apart from the four nawab begums, earlier too when Bhopal was just a newly founded independent kingdom, the state had actually been ruled successively by two women—the "unofficial" nawab begums. The first one was Fateh Bibi, the Rajput princess and wife of Nawab Dost Mohammad Khan (Bhopal's founder and ruler; 1723-1728), the other was the universally respected Maaji Mamola Bai, wife of Nawab Yar Mohammad Khan (1728-1742), also a Rajput princess of Kota. Though not overtly rulers of the state, these two astute and intuitive ladies exercised great influence in effecting proper discharge of governance of the state affairs through their husbands, the ruling nawabs. A kind-hearted motherly figure to one and all, Mamola Bai earned the love and respectof her subjects and was thus addressed and referred to as *Maaji* (Dear Mother). Mamola Bai was the daughter of the Rajput king of Kota; according to some historians, she possibly belonged to a noble Brahmin family of northern India. Courageous and competent, she had taken over the reins of the kingdom after the death of her husband. But a daring Sultan Mohammad, half-brother of the late Nawab, challenged her claiming the throne for himself. Assisted by his younger brother Sadar Mohammad he seized the fort of Fatehgarh declaring himself the new succeeding nawab. An undaunted Mamola Bai, then positioned in the old citadel of Islamnagar, faced the revolt. She publicly proclaimed her stepson, 11-year-old Faiz Mohammad Khan, the eldest child of her late husband, as the only lawful heir to the throne. Thereafter she boldly commandeered a force of 5,000 troops headed by her trusted lieutenant Vijai Ram to quell the revolt. The rebelling Sultan Mohammad together with his brother Sadar Mohammad had to surrender unconditionally after a severe confrontation, near Idgah Hills.

However, the young Nawab Faiz Mohammad even after achieving adulthood turned out to be more inclined towards spirituality than in the affairs of the state governance. So Maaji Mamola once again had to take over the reins and as the regent of Faiz she governed the state most competently. During her rule, Bhopal signed a treaty with the Maratha Peshwas and also took control over the politically sensitive Raisen Fort, having obtained a sanction from the Mughal court at Delhi. But in 1777 came another crisis when Faiz died issuless at an early age. Sensing another problem in the line of succession Maaji Mamola declared Faiz's younger brother Hayat Mohammad Khan as the Nawab of Bhopal. Since he was a minor, Mamola Bai continued to function as his regent ruling the state as before.

However, it may be said that the only real and major confrontation in the history of Fatehgarh (Bhopal) took place during the years 1812–1813 under the reign of Nawab Ghous Mohammad Khan, the successor of Hayat Mohammad. An overwhelming united, 82000-strong army, from the Maratha states of Nagpur and Gwalior had together invaded Bhopal. Leading the forces were the two veteran generals of Scindia, Jagua Bapu and Kachua Bapu, known for their ferocity as well as cunning, who laid almost a year-long siege on the citadel of Fatehgarh. Other than the lakes they surrounded the capital from all sides, isolating Fatehgarh from the rest of the country. The siege, almost a catastrophe, was a turning point in the history of Bhopal; it did bring out the best as well as the worst of the men in the garrison who mattered most for Bhopal in distress. Treachery had played its role when the men guarding the fort's Budhwara Gate were lured with money as a price for throwing the gate open before the Maratha forces. However, the dutiful commander Bakhshi Bahadur assisted by a few Pathan soldiers defended the fort with exemplary courage until the General Nawab Wazir Mohammad Khan (then ruler in opposition) arrived with additional forces. Bakhshi was grievously injured in the skirmish and so was Moiz Mohammad (son of Nawab Ghous Mohammad Khan), but none of them relented until the invaders retreated back. All the residents of the fort, the women too, resisted the siege with all their might and in every possible way. The women shedding their purdah and dressed like men showered stones and boiling water on the enemy from the rampart; some even fired guns and canons to assist their male counterparts. But Nawab Ghous Mohammad Khan, a lethargic and timid person, shied away from the raging battle. He prefered a truce or even a surrender to the enemy; but his wife Zeenat Begum and child daughter Gohar Ara (later known as Nawab Qudsia Begum) held on, helping the fighting men to guard the fort. In fact, this mother and daughter duo had been leading and inspiring the other women for taking part in the battle. It is said that Zeenat Begum herself fired canons when both Bakhshi and Moiz lay injured. Even the Bourbons—the two daring French—Inayat Masih (Salvador de Bourbon) and his son Shahzad Masih (Balthazar de Bourbon) fought side by side with Wazir Mohammad Khan and son Nazar Mohammad. This was the occasion for these French royalty to pay back the debt that they owed to the late Maaji Mamola who had earlier sheltered them when they fled to Bhopal being in distress. Unfortunately, the citadel Fatehgarh did not have enough store of provision to tide over such a prolonged period of crisis; other than the regular inmates the garrison also had 11,000 fighting troops to be fed. The daring Bakhshi and the Bourbons used to smuggle in food sent by loyal Rajput zamindars; it involved taking great risks, such as swimming across the lake in midnight, but the quantity of food thus procured was hardly sufficient. Out of hunger the people had to eat "gutkhas" made of crushed tamarind seeds wrapped and roasted in some edible leaves (the customary practice of consuming specially made Bhopali Gutkha as mouth freshener has continued since then). Finally, when the stock of arms and ammunitions too fell short, even the valiant general Wazir Mohammad became disheartened. After consulting his trusted associates he was sadly contemplating surrender. Legend has it that at this crucial stage he went to pay a visit to the revered Pir Mastan Shah (his grave is located just outside Sadar Manzil palace which presently houses the head office of the Bhopal Municipal Corporation). Wazir Mohammad thought of seeking the blessings of the Pir before sending his emissary to negotiate with the Marathas about the terms of surrender of Fatehgarh. In full reverence he placed his sword and turban at the feet of the saint submitting that he was unable to fight any longer for want of food, arms and ammunitions. On hearing him, the Pir went into a short trance, then pointing towards a dark secluded spot he asked the Nawab to dig the place. After little excavation came out a huge cache of explosives and weapons; all these had been securely stored there by the late Nawab Yar Mohammad Khan, the great grandfather of Wazir. The musings on surrender was at once averted, and the brave and exulted Nawab Wazir Mohammad, after nine long months of weary deprivations, decided to go for the final "do or die" battle. Guns roared once again followed by a vigorous charge on the enemies. Jagua Bapu's unwary army retreated back in great haste, his soldiers were already sick and weakened due to a violent epidemic of cholera while the utterly demoralised Kachua Bapu committed suicide as his fleeing forces left him abandoned. Thus, instead of surrender the valiant Nawab Wazir Mohammad had won a glorious and most significant victory in one of the historic battles fought in central India—the only real battle ever fought in Bhopal. After this war of siege the Nawab had ultimately created a strong posse of regular army to defend Bhopal against the ever-invading Marathas. Later, during the 1830s the ruling Nawab Jahangir Mohammad Khan established the cantonment of Jahangirabad around Fatehgarh.

In the meantime, desirous of wresting power in central India, the British too became involved in a series of serious confrontations with the Marathas. In the first Anglo-Maratha war that took place in 1778, British General Thomas Goddard campaigned in central India. Bhopal's Nawab Hayat Mohammad Khan sided with him expecting in return the friendship of the British and their assistance in getting rid of the marauding Marathas. But his expectations remained unfulfilled as the situations in central India were volatile and Goddard could not really trust the Nawab either. However, in the third Anglo-Maratha War of 1817 the British had won decisively and consolidated their position in central India. Thereafter a treaty of dependence had been signed between Nawab Ghous Mohammad Khan and the British Government (East India Company). Accordingly, the independent kingdom of Bhopal earned the much-coveted friendship of the British. Though purchased under tutelage, this bond of friendship lasted till the year 1947 when India won freedom from the British rule. In 1818 was signed another treaty between ruler Nazar Mohammad Khan, the then nawab and the East India Company by which Bhopal attained the status of a princely state in British India. Under terms of the treaty the state of Bhopal also included Raisen and Sehore districts forming the Central India Agency; it spanned over the Vindhya Range with its northern area lying on the Malwa Plateau while the southern portion lay in the valley of the river Narmada that formed the state boundary. Bhopal became the administrative sector of this Central India Agency.

However, since the treaty of 1818, Bhopal under British protection was spared the constant apprehension of enemy attacks; a great boon for the reigning nawabs no doubt. It was also a smooth sailing since then with effective administration of state affairs that had been wanting so long. Such days of peace and tranquility augmented a long spell of glorious regime under the four consecutive women rulers—the nawab begums, under whose care Bhopal had flowered into prosperity. It was a long tenure extending over a century during which the four famous aristocratic ladies from the royal family managed the state affairs with utmost efficiency. Their balanced and impartial rule led to the rise of a unique amalgamation of cultures in Bhopal; side by side with the Muslims, the Hindus too were given important administrative positions in management of the state. This had instilled not only a sense of social harmony, but also mutual respect and tolerance for religions, thus encouraging a cosmopolitan culture. Perhaps, it is for this cultural psyche lasting over centuries in the minds of the local population that Bhopal has never witnessed any instance of communal violence so far.

Of the four women rulers the first official nawab begum was Nawab Qudsia Begum. Also known by the name Gohar Ara Begum she was the daughter of Nawab Ghous Mohammad Khan. In 1817, aged 16 she was married to Nawab Nazar Mohammad Khan, son of Wazir Mohammad Khan who became the Nawab of Bhopal superseding his predecessor, the feeble-minded and incompetent Nawab Ghous. After the death of Wazir his son Nazar had succeeded as nawab in the face of enmity and several secret conspiracies against him. Finally, in 1819 just two years after his marriage with Qudsia Begum, Nawab Nazar Mohammad was assassinated by some unknown assailant. This was indeed a stunning blow to the royal family as well as for the state. A great deal of controversy arose about succession to Bhopal's throne, since within the large royal family there were more than eighty contenders in various orders of claims to the throne. The principal

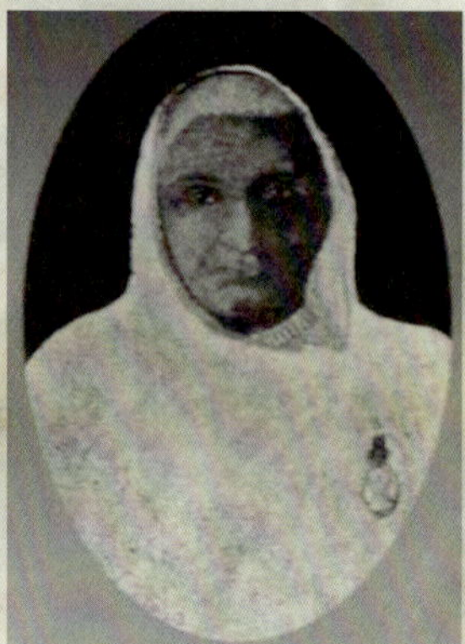

Nawab Qudsia Begum

contenders numbering nearly twenty, prepared for a protracted battle on the issue; they all had assembled at the "Durbar Hall" to attend the mourning rite for the dead; it was also the venue where the crucial matter of selecting the next ruler was to be decided. The hall was full with royal family members, high-ranking officials, religious functionaries like the Qazi and the Mufti as well as the British political agent, Major Henley. As the vital issue of inheritance was being discussed, the 18-year-old widow of Nawab Nazar Mohammad, Qudsia Begum, took off her veils and clasping the 15-month-old baby daughter Sikandar to her breast, moved to the centre of the hall in a calm and dignified gait. Addressing the big gathering she produced the will of her husband which clearly ordained that in the event of his premature death his minor daughter Sikandar would be the successor of the kingdom of Bhopal while his wife Qudsia would rule as the regent until Sikandar got married to a "close family member" who would become Bhopal's ruling nawab thereafter. Nobody dared to object the statement, neither any of the contenders had the courage to challenge the will of the late Nawab, since such a challenge was likely to indirectly identify the real culprit behind the killing of Nawab Nazar Mohammad. All high-ranking loyal officials as well as the Qazi and the Mufti having supported the testament and with the nod of Major Henley, the issue was decided finally in favour of Qudsia Begum. She took over the reins of the kingdom as Nawab Qudsia Begum, the regent on behalf of her minor daughter Sikandar.

Thus, in the history of Bhopal, began the reign of the nawab begums which continued uninterruptedly for 107 years. Beginning with Nawab Qudsia Begum there were three other succeeding nawab begums; they all proved their mettle in governance as well as in various aspects of the development of the state continuing throughout their reign—almost equalling the total tenure of their predecessors, the eight male nawabs.

Nawab Qudsia Begum, though illiterate, had sharp intelligence and foresight. Brave and ahead of her times, she refused to follow the tradition of purdah for the women, an unthinkable act for a Muslim lady in those days; but she possessed such a strong personality that none of the male members in the family or royal household dared to challenge her. In fact, the other women rulers after her, derived inspiration from the upright character of Qudsia and the trends she had set were regarded as precedents. In spite of all her firmness Qudsia Begum also possessed genuine concern for her subjects; it is said that she would not take dinner unless being informed that all her people have had their food as well. Both her daughter Sikandar Jahan as well as grand-daughter Shah Jahan had been trained and mentored by her to become future nawab begums—worthy as well as capable of independent state governance. Being the first ruling Begum of Bhopal, rather the first lady in the Islamic history of India as the Head of a State, she often displayed her military skills—using weapons, riding horses and elephants—to silence the men who were doubtful of her competence to govern the kingdom. But soon her critics were all convinced that she was the right person to lead the country both in war and peace. Her acute political foresight finds expression when, defying all sorts of oppositions raised from various quarters, she sided with the British during the great 1857 uprising of the Indian army. A biography of the Begum *Hayat-i-Qudsia* narrates intimate personal accounts of her life. It mentions that Begum Qudsia, highly concerned about her subjects, used to visit the homes of the poor to inquire after their welfare and always extended the necessary help and advice to the needy families. Leading a simple and austere life, she was kind-hearted by nature and was known to have been donating grants impartially to Muslims and Hindus alike. That is why she was often fondly compared and regarded by her subjects as the incarnation of late Maaji Mamola, the loving motherly soul. Her pious charity had extended to as far as Saudi Arabia in those days. She donated a large sum of money for necessary constructions of *rubaat* (guest houses) at the holy centres of Mecca and Medina for the accommodation of the Haj pilgrims arriving from Bhopal.

As the regent of Sikandar, her minor daughter, Qudsia Begum successfully ruled Bhopal from the year 1819 till 1837. After Sikandar Begum's marriage in 1835, the son-in-law Jahangir Mohammad Khan became the nawab as was ordained in the terms of the will of late Nawab Nazar Mohammad Khan. However, after the premature death of Jahangir in 1844, Qudsia once again became the ruler as well as the first Nawab Begum of Bhopal; this happened at the behest of the British, in appreciation of the abilities and cooperative spirit perceived in her past performances. She had ruled creditably till the year 1860 before abdicating in favour of her daughter Sikandar.

The salient features of Qudsia's administration were the laying of the foundation of waterworks and pipelines throughout the state. This complicated as well as extensive work had been entrusted to an experienced Scottish engineer David Cook. For the construction and expansion of railways she had granted 15 Lakh rupees—an enormous sum by the standards those days. As an efficient ruler of the princely state under British India, as well as for her whole-hearted cooperation with the British all along, she had been specially invited to Lord Lytton's "durbar" in 1876, when Queen Victoria was being proclaimed as the Empress of India, and honoured with the "Order of the Crown of India". The Jama Masjid in the heart of the city was constructed by her in 1837. She also built a beautiful palace by the name Gohar Mahal, which is a magnificent embodiment of the fusion of Hindu and Islamic architecture. Another architectural marvel, the Shaukat Mahal too had been constructed during her reign by a team of foreign architects and builders under the guidance of some Frenchmen connected with the Bourbon royalty of France.

Next in line, Nawab Sikandar Jahan Begum, courageous and firm like her mother, too never observed purdah. Moulded by mother Qudsia, she was trained in horse riding, archery, shooting and other martial arts. In 1835 she married Jahangir Mohammad Khan, a close relative, but unfortunately it was not a happy marriage; their relationship soon became strained as the husband Jahangir was an orthodox chauvinist. Though he had acquired the throne of nawab by virtue of his marriage, he was too demanding and insisted on his wife Sikandar observing the tradition of purdah as was the custom for Muslim women those days, which she refused to comply with. In 1838 was born their

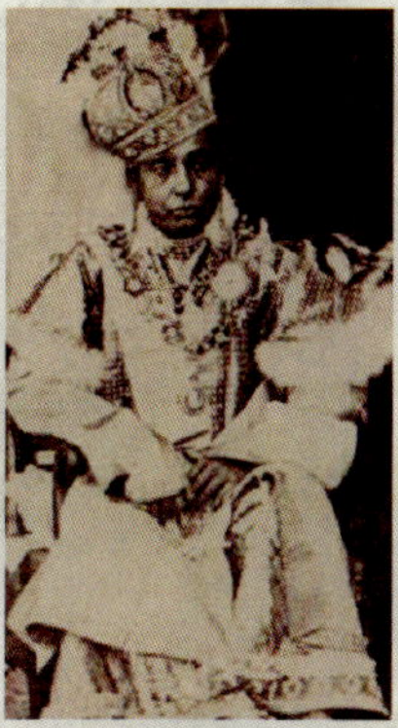

Nawab Sikandar Jahan Begum

daughter Shah Jahan, but the increasing bitterness in conjugal relations forced Sikandar to move out of the Islamnagar Fort. With her child daughter and mother Qudsia Begum she shifted to the citadel of Fatehgarh (Bhopal). After the death of Nawab Jahangir Khan in 1844, once again at the insistence of the British, Qudsia Begum was reinstated as the Nawab of Bhopal. However, in 1860 Qudsia abdicated in favour of Sikandar who thereafter ruled as the succeeding nawab begum till 1868.

Sikandar Begum, the new nawab begum was instrumental in effecting reforms in civil administration. New roads with lamp posts for night illumination were laid out in and around the city. Needy people were given financial assistence to improve their standard of living. While reforming the police system it was arranged that each area had to be supervised by an efficient *thanedar* (officer). The Begum also ushered in several vital reforms in the royal Bhopal army and spent a sum of two lakh rupees on its modernization. Barracks were built for the soldiers, new arms and weapons were procured and soldiers were sent to nearby Sehore for training in the skills of modern warfare.

Sikandar brought out judicial legislations too by codifying the laws and establishing separate courts for the trial of civil and criminal cases. Also inducted were separate laws for the Hindu and Muslim communities. Various other reforms were made in the field of education as well. In addition to vernaculars and written languages she also made English and Mathematics compulsory subjects to be taught in schools. The beautiful Moti Masjid (Pearl Mosque) as well as the Moti Mahal Palace were built during her time. Like her mother Qudsia Begum, Sikandar too had aligned with the British helping them to crush the 1857 revolt of the Indian soldiers, notwithstanding the severe opposition from various quarters of religious fundamentalists. Later, after peace was restored the British had conferred on her the title "Order of the Star of India".

In 1863 Nawab Sikandar Jahan Begum accompanied by her mother Qudsia went for a pilgrimage to Mecca. On their way they spent a few days in Turkey as the honourable guest of Sultan Abdul Hameed. The Sultan had warned them beforehand about the risks of journey from Mecca to Medina since the route was infested with dreaded bandits. Moreover words had already spread across the country about the wealth and valuables that the begums had been carrying with them. It so happened that the begums had helped some Siddi Arabs in Turkey and saved their leader Hazrat Bilal who had been condemned to death. Exercising her great personal influence Sikandar Begum had secured his release, and the ever-grateful Bilal offered to escort the begums ensuring their safe passage to Medina. But as apprehended, en route some miscreants had kidnapped Sikandar after overpowering Bilal and his men. Immediately Bilal rushed to the Sultan for help. The Sultan sent some soldiers under Maulvi Ilmas, another Siddi Arab and a brave warrior. In the skirmish that followed, six of Bilal's men lost their life but the Begum had been rescued. At the Begum's behest Bilal and his party accompanied them all the way till they reached back to Bhopal safely. The Arabs were then sheltered close to the palace of Nawab Sikandar Begum and had been entrusted with the great responsibility of guarding the rulers of Bhopal.

Nawab Sikandar Jahan Begum died in 1868 and was laid to rest in her beautiful garden Farhat Afzah. Thereafter began the rule of

Nawab Shah Jahan Begum, the third successive Nawab Begum of Bhopal. She was the only surviving child of Sikandar Begum and Nawab Jahangir Khan. After Jahangir's death in 1844, at the age of six years she was recognised as the ruler of Bhopal, but during her minority her grandmother functioned as the regent. However, in 1860 the British recognised her mother Sikandar Begum as the rightful ruler of the state. So, Shah Jahan's claim to the throne had been kept in abeyance and she succeeded as the nawab begum only after the mother's death.

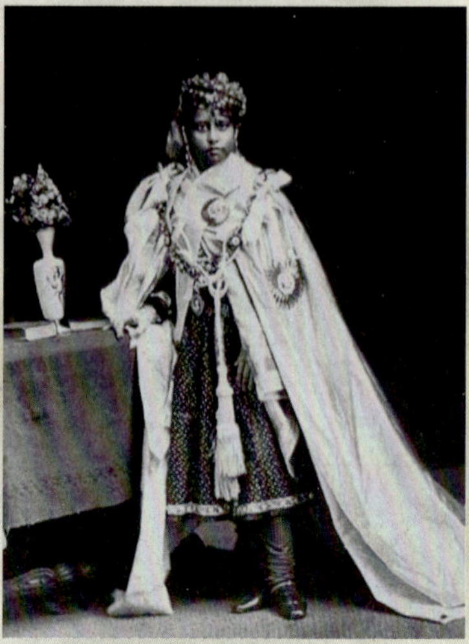
Nawab Shah Jahan Begum

Like her mother, Shah Jahan too had been groomed by her grandmother Qudsia Begum, in military as well as in administrative skills befitting a ruler. Side by side she had also developed a taste for literature and fine arts and later went on to author several books. Nawab Sikandar Begum was keen that her only child and the heir apparent to the throne of Bhopal, daughter Shah Jahan, should learn poetry and music simultaneously with acquiring skills in martial arts and state administration.

Nawab Shah Jahan Begum brought about several improvements in the various administrative procedures. She reformed the revenue and taxation systems and effected substantial gains in the financial position of the state. To facilitate irrigation and water supply, a lake had been excavated and a dam was built too. The police force was rejuvenated to improve its efficiency; soldiers got higher salary, modern weapons and improved military training. To strengthen state budget, the government resorted to farming of opium. For the first time a census of the population had been undertaken under her rule. She had also granted a large sum of money for expansion of the railways; the Itarsi, Bhopal and Bhilsa, Gwalior lines were laid during her time. Shah Jahan Begum was also passionate about architecture. Concentrating on the development of the area north of the walled city Fatehgarh she established a new city and named it Shahjahanabad. It was perhaps one amongst the few planned localities of India in those days. The new city had accommodations for different classes of citizens pursuing different professions. Besides her own palace, Taj Mahal, there was Barah Mahal, Ali Manzil, Benazir Palace, Mughalpura, Amir Ganj, Nematpura and the Nawab Manzil too. Construction of the imposing Taj-ul-Masajid, the grandest landmark of Bhopal was initiated by her, though unfortunately she died before its completion. Shah Jahan Begum's famous Taj Mahal Palace complex is another architectural marvel of Bhopal. Under her rule the state economy had flourished and Bhopal came to be known for its finely crafted artifacts like delicate art jewellery and zari (zardozi) works made with gold sequins. It was during her reign that postage stamps of Bhopal was first issued in 1876. To facilitate trade and commerce in the state she had judiciously introduced the coins and currency of British India discarding those of Bhopal. Because of the overcrowding in Sadar Manzil, the hall of her public audience, the venue was later shifted to the newly built Minto Hall. The famed Minto Hall later had served as the Vidhan Sabha of the newly formed state of Madhya Pradesh for forty years, from 1956 till 1996. The Begum also had founded the

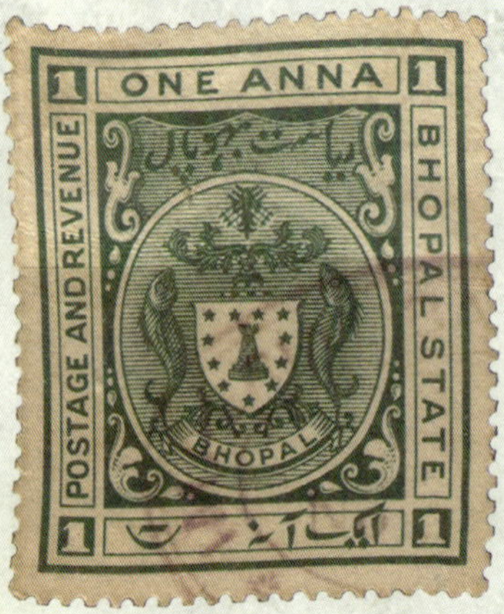

Postage stamp issued by Shah Jahan Begum

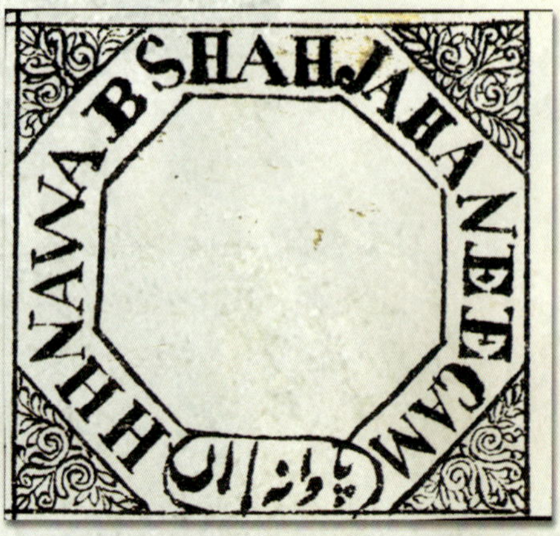

Postage Stamp of Bhopal

King George Hospital which is now the main government hospital renamed as the Hamidia Hospital.

Known for her piety and benevolence Nawab Shah Jahan Begum donated a huge sum of money for building a mosque at Woking, Surrey, in the United Kingdom. She also granted a sizable amount towards founding the Mohammadan Anglo-Oriental College at Aligarh which in later years greatly flourished and turned out to become the renowned Aligarh Muslim University.

In 1855 Nawab Shah Jahan Begum married Baqi Khan, a middle order nobleman who died in 1867. Four years later she married once again but did not beget any children out of this second marriage. After her death she was succeeded by her only surviving issue, daughter Sultan Jahan who was born out of the first wedlock; soon after birth, Sultan Jahan was declared the heir apparent who eventually went on to become the fourth successive Nawab Begum of Bhopal.

An accomplished lady, Sultan Jahan (also called Kaikhusrau and Sarkar Amma) Begum was known for her learning. She had written in Urdu her autobiography detailing the way of life in Bhopal during her time. She will ever be remembered for her great contributions in the field of education, for women in particular; she had made basic education freely available for everybody in Bhopal, almost a century ago. Schools and technical institutes were set up where qualified teachers had been employed. From 1920 until her death in 1930 she had functioned as the founding Chancellor of the Aligarh Muslim University—the only woman to hold that office till this day. In 1914 she had been elected as president of All India Muslim Ladies' Association. Greatly concerned about public health and hygiene she improved the water supply system and strongly advocated vaccination as well as mass inoculation programmes and had established a municipal body to look after public works, health and hygiene. Nawab Sultan Jahan had also introduced far-reaching reforms in taxation, judiciary, police, prison, and in the army. She had improved agricultural activities too by promoting better irrigation and construction of small lakes and dams. For the eradication of corruption in the judiciary as well as in the revenue departments she had recruited many officers even from outside the state. Such a step was indeed very much necessary, though her actions in this regard were vehemently opposed by those having vested interests in the whole system of unscrupulous profiteering and led to widespread political agitations. Being a democratic at heart she had established the Majlis Mashwara, a general assembly of the elected legislative members, to enact new laws that would benefit the existing social order. Although, her own palace was Sadar Manzil in Bhopal, (presently the head office of Bhopal Municipal Corporation), she had developed her own mini-city Ahmedabad, named after her late

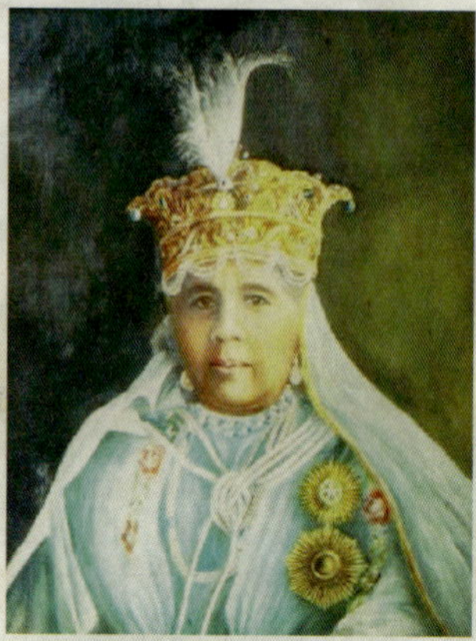
Nawab Sultan Jahan Begum

husband Ahmed Khan. There too she built the charming palace Qasr-e-Sultani (later, Ahmedabad Palace), which presently houses the Saifia College. Soon Ahmedabad turned out to become a posh residential area as the royalty and the elite gradually started moving there. A beautiful garden was developed there named Jai-up-Abser where the Begum had installed the first water pump. Another palace, the Noor-us-Sabah constructed there, is now a grand heritage hotel. Earlier it was the haveli of Nawab Hamidullah Khan who bequeathed the palace to his eldest daughter Abida Begum. Nawab Sultan Jahan is also credited with the contribution of a large amount towards the revival and restoration of the old and damaged stupas and other Buddhist relics of Sanchi. Her benevolence in this regard proved the generous outlook and permissiveness as was being followed by her predecessors in their attempt to bring about religious integration.

In 1911 Nawab Sultan Jahan was returning from her tour to Europe via Turkey; on this occasion Sultan Mehmet Reshad of Turkey was to bestow upon her the rare honour of "Devlet Nishan", the country's highest award. But the British then having strained relations with Turkey, advised her not to accept the award. Miffed by the British intervention, the Sultan had presented the Begum a much more precious gift—the Moi-e-Mukaddas, a sacred hair of the Prophet. So, after the Hazratbal shrine of Kashmir, Bhopal is the only other state in India possessing the holy relic of Prophet Mohammad. This most precious of royal treasures was then preserved by the Nawab Begum in a very special room of her palace. The relic is displayed once a year at Ibrahimpura while parts of it are also preserved in Ahmedabad Palace as well as in the holy dargah at Peer Gate.

In 1926, after a glorious reign spanning 25 years, Nawab Sultan Jahan Begum abdicated the throne in favour of her youngest child and only surviving son, Hamidullah Khan. And thus ended the 107-year long uninterrupted rule of the nawab begums in Bhopal; their regime, regarded in Indian history as the golden period of regency of the royal Pathan dynasty and the kingdom founded by Dost Mohammad Khan.

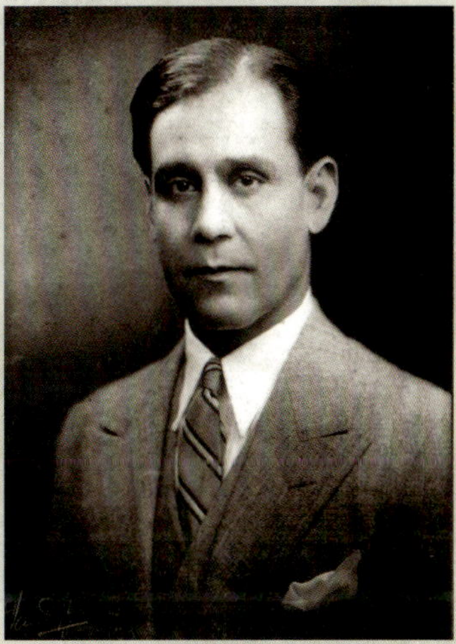

Nawab Hamidullah Khan, the last ruling nawab

Nawab Hamidullah Khan had three daughters. The eldest princess Abida Sultan was the heir apparent of the kingdom. She had been brought up and trained by her grandmother Sultan Jahan Begum as a devout lady, though by nature she had the mould of a strongly independent personality. Abida grew up as a perfect sports-woman from her childhood; at the age of 8 she became an expert horse rider and soon after she joined her father's polo team. She was also fond of hunting wild animals and had bagged 73 tiger kills at a very young age. She could very well play the manly games of hockey and cricket and was a squash as well as swimming champion too. Speed driving cars was her fascination and she was the second woman in India to get a pilot's license which she secured after running away from home!

When India was partitioned in 1947 Abida fell strongly against the merger of Bhopal with the Indian Union. She had declined to succeed her father just to be merely the titular Nawab of Bhopal without the real power to rule. A staunch supporter of Mohammad Ali Jinnah, she chose to migrate to Pakistan. She had represented Pakistan at the United Nations and had served as Pakistan's ambassador in Brazil and Chile.

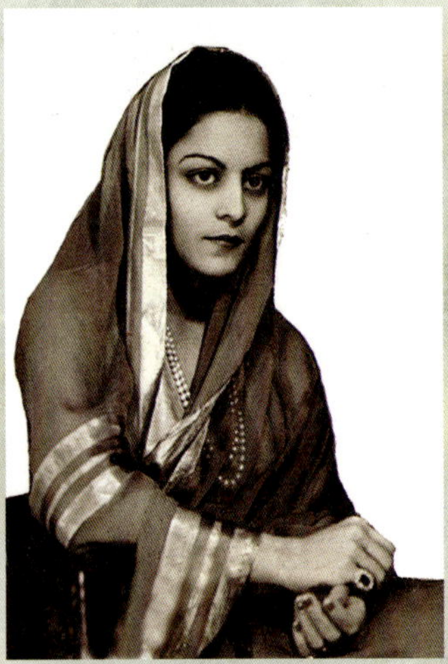

Begum Sajida Sultan

After Abida's exit from Bhopal her younger sister Sajida, then already married into the Pataudi family, became the heir apparent and succeeded her father Nawab Hamidullah Khan in 1960. As Nawab Sajida Sultan Begum she remained the titular Nawab of Bhopal till death, after which her son "Tiger" Mansoor Ali Khan Pataudi, the world-famous cricketer succeeded as the Nawab. He had married the celebrated film actress Sharmila Tagore of a Bengali family. Mansoor Ali Khan died in 2011 leaving behind a son and two daughters.

Modern History

Since the early 20th century, struggle for independence and protests against the ruthless exploitation of the country by the ruling British Raj had become rife in India. Led by Mahatma Gandhi and many other national figures, Indians had been agitating fiercely to get rid of the shackles of British rule. The country-wide agitation had cast its shadow on the princely states too. Finally in 1947 India achieved freedom from foreign rule to become an independent democratic republic. Prior to India's independence Nawab Hamidullah Khan had signed the Instrument of Accession, making Bhopal a part of free India. Later however, he had expressed his opinion to retain Bhopal as a self-ruled separate unit of India; the change in his stance was resented not only by the Indian leaders but by the nationalist figures of Bhopal also. Agitations broke out against the Nawab which led to the arrests of many prominent Bhopali leaders including Shankar Dayal Sharma and several noted Muslim personalities. But the firm measures taken by the Government of India finally compelled Nawab Hamidullah to sign the agreement effecting Bhopal's merger with the Indian Union in 1949. Thereafter, according to the States

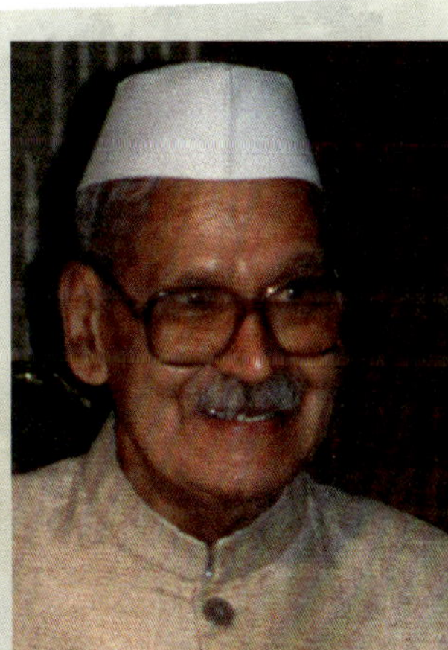

Shankar Dayal Sharma, a political leader from Bhopal, who served as the President of India from 1992 to 1997

Reorganisation Act of 1956, Bhopal was integrated into the state of Madhya Pradesh.

During the years of India's struggle for independence several firebrand nationalists and freedom fighters fled the country hoping to avail foreign assistance to dislodge the British from India. Two such freedom-seeking and leading patriotic figures hailing from Bhopal, Rafiq Ahmad Khan or "Roosi" and Abdul Hafiz Mohammad Barkatullah or "Bhopali", had established close ties with the Amir of Afghanistan and later with the Marxist revolutionary and Soviet leader Vladimir Ilyich Lenin. During World War I both of them fled the country; Barkatullah went to Kabul while Roosi had left for Moscow where in 1916 was formed the Provisional Government of India (in exile) with Maulana Barkatullah nominated as the first prime minister, Raja Mahendra Pratap as the president and Maulana Ubaidullah as the home minister. The newly formed provisional Indian Government received financial support from the Soviets but no military assistance was available. In 1927 Barkatullah died in San Francisco. In his honour the University of Bhopal was renamed in 1988 as Barkatullah University.

After the formation of Madhya Pradesh in 1956 there was a tie between the cities of Jabalpur, Indore, Gwalior and Bhopal each of them seeking to be crowned as the capital of the large newly formed state. Bhopal's claim was given top priority, the proposal being put forward and backed by Syed Zahoor Hashmi, an eminent political leader. Hashmi presented Bhopal's case to the central committee that was assigned the task of selecting a suitable capital for the new state. In his meticulous arguments Hashmi convinced the authority that from various considerations, such as the geographical significance, social culture, communal harmony, religious freedom and architectural heritage, Bhopal scores over the others to deserve the status of the ideal administrative capital of Madhya Pradesh. Playing an important role in it was Shankar Dayal Sharma, then chief minister of the newly formed state; at his behest Pandit Govind Ballav Pant had recommended Bhopal's name to Prime Minister Jawaharlal Nehru. But ultimately it was Nawab Hamidullah's friendship with Nehru that succeeded in securing the honour of the pride of the place for Bhopal as the capital city of Madhya Pradesh.

A composite view

Royal Architectural Marvels

When Raja Bhoj created the lakes Bhopal was a non-descript village. With the passage of time the village grew up and expanded, largely around the lakes. During the rule of the Gond king Nizam Shah in the early 1700s, Bhopal became a semi-urban, prosperous locality where the lone architectural marvel was Rani Kamlapati's huge elegant palace. The most striking feature of the seven-storey palace was that it had been constructed right on top of the 700-year-old check dam built by Raja Bhoj. The dam site separating the Upper and the Lower Lakes was called Tila Tanha by Raja Bhoj. Nizam Shah built the palace for his beloved wife, the beautiful Rani Kamlapati, which however lay deserted after the death of the Rani. The remains of the 300-year-old dilapidated palace are supposedly the earliest trace of significant architecture in Bhopal. The area is still known as the Purana Quila (of Nizam Shah) at Kamla Park.

Large portions of this abandoned palace were later pulled down in 1911 for widening of the road under the planning and supervision of British engineer John Lockwood Kipling (father of Rudyard Kipling), when Nawab Sultan Jahan Begum was the ruler of Bhopal. What remains of the ruined palace today is just the royal bath area.

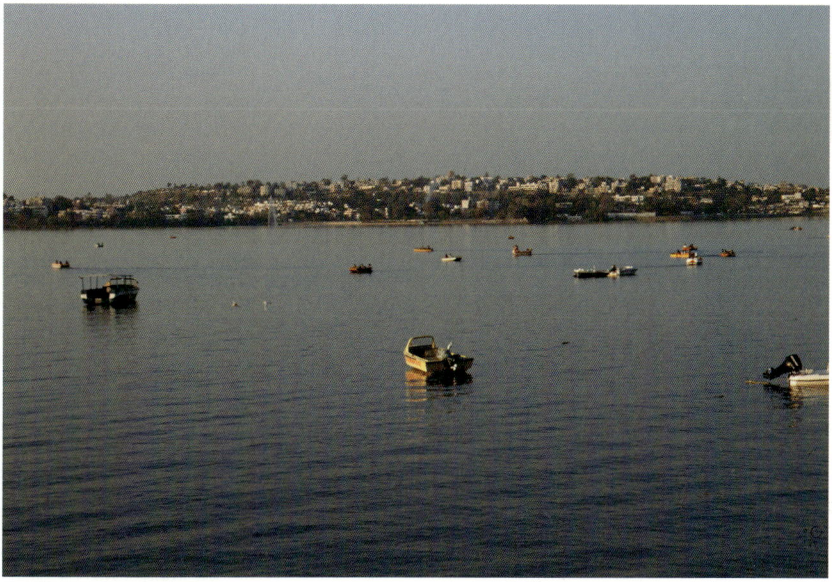

A view of the city of Bhopal across the Upper Lake

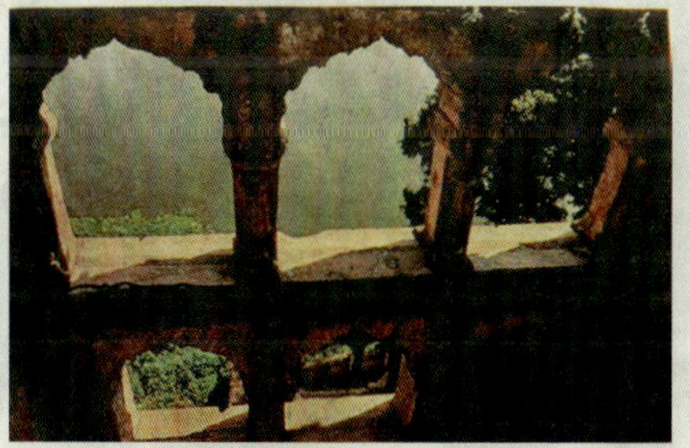

Ruins of Kamlapati Palace

Presently, the main part of the dilapidated Kamlapati Palace houses the local office of the Archaeological Survey of India. A long flight of stairs leads to the lowest floor through a gallery of stone arches reaching the ghats on the waterfront, where in the remote past Rani Kamlapati used to take her bath and enjoy swimming in the company of her ladies-in-waiting. The place is now known as Kamla Park.

Dost Mohammad Khan's original capital was Islamnagar (earlier Jagdishpur) near Berasia in the outskirts of Bhopal. The fortified

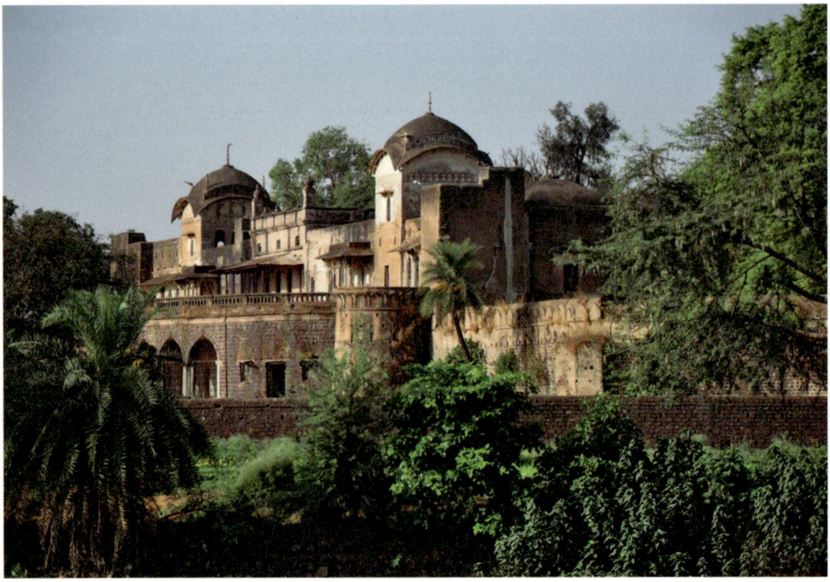

Islamnagar

citadel contained the famous garden palace Chaman Mahal, the second-oldest architectural heritage in Bhopal. Built in 1715 with sandstone, bricks and lime, the palace and garden complex is surrounded by two high compound walls. The landscaping of the gardens follow the style of the famous Mughal gardens of Pinjore and those in Kashmir. The complex has an exclusive underground water system which still has a water heating arrangement as was used for the hamam or the royal bath. Islamnagar has two other palaces—the Rani Mahal and the Gond Mahal. The varied architectures of these structures on the whole represents a fusion of the Mughal, Rajput and Gond styles.

After usurping the kingdom of the Gond Rani Kamlapati in 1723, Dost Mohammad had refurbished his new acquisition, the territory of Bhopal, in a big way, naming it Fatehgarh, his second citadel. The entire city or "Sahar-i-Khas" was enclosed within a high protective wall 6 km long. With the expansion of the city during the rule of the nawab begums, the surrounding city wall too was gradually extended further by another 10 km. The wall at Dost Mohammad's time had seven gates in all, starting from the fort and ending at the Upper Lake; of those only the Jumerati Gate remains today. Around the royal garden square called Khirniwala Maidan, four gates were built during the rule of the nawab begums, for the royal palaces, of which the gates for Shaukat Mahal, Sadar Manzil and Moti Mahal now survive. Along with these also exist four other gates, namely the Kala Darwaza, Taj Mahal Gate, Military Gate and Shahjahanabad Gate. Thus fortified, the Fatehgarh Fort had, for over 150 years, saved the city from marauding invaders, mainly the Marathas. While inaugurating the Kasturba Gandhi Medical College in 1963 Jawaharlal Nehru had noticed that a huge wall was being hammered down to make room for constructions of the college. Realising the importance of the historic fort as well as of the imposing magnificence of the great wall, he advised against further demolition and emphasised on the preservation of the old citadel, which happens to be the largest of the living heritage sites in the capital city.

Perhaps, the most important architectural heritage site in the city is the elegant palace Shaukat Mahal located near the crowded Chowk Bazar area. Built in 1830, it is one

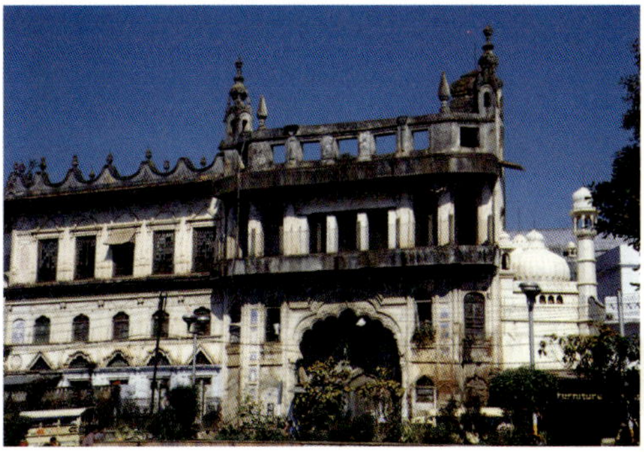

Shaukat Mahal designed by a descendant of the Bourbon brothers

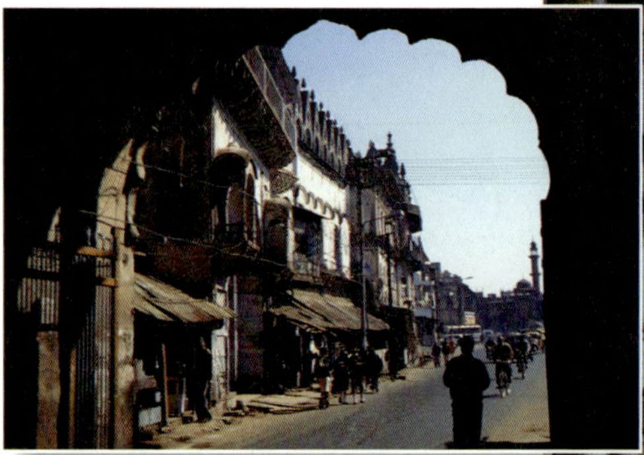

An alley in Old Bhopal through the Shaukat Mahal and Sadar Manzil gateway

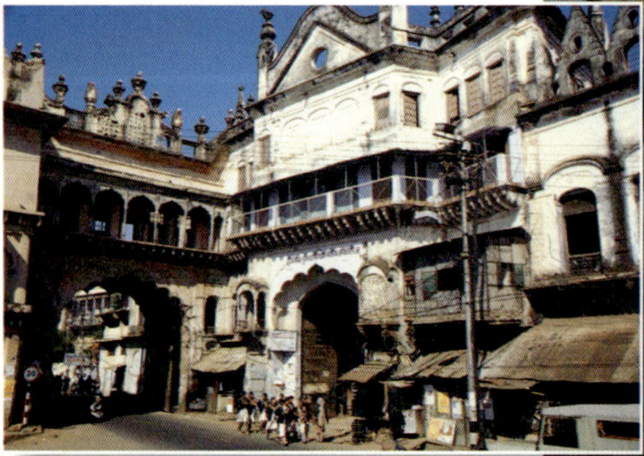

Sadar Manzil alongside the Fatehgarh gateway

Right: Iqbal Maidan and Palace, Moti Mahal, Fatehgarh gateway and Sadar Manzil, Old Bhopal

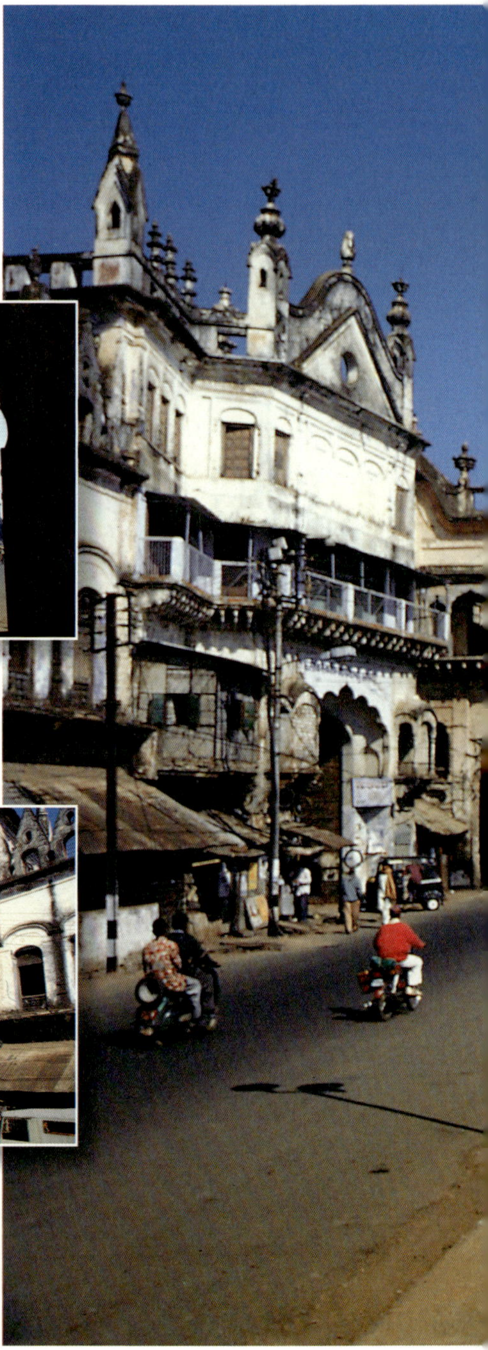

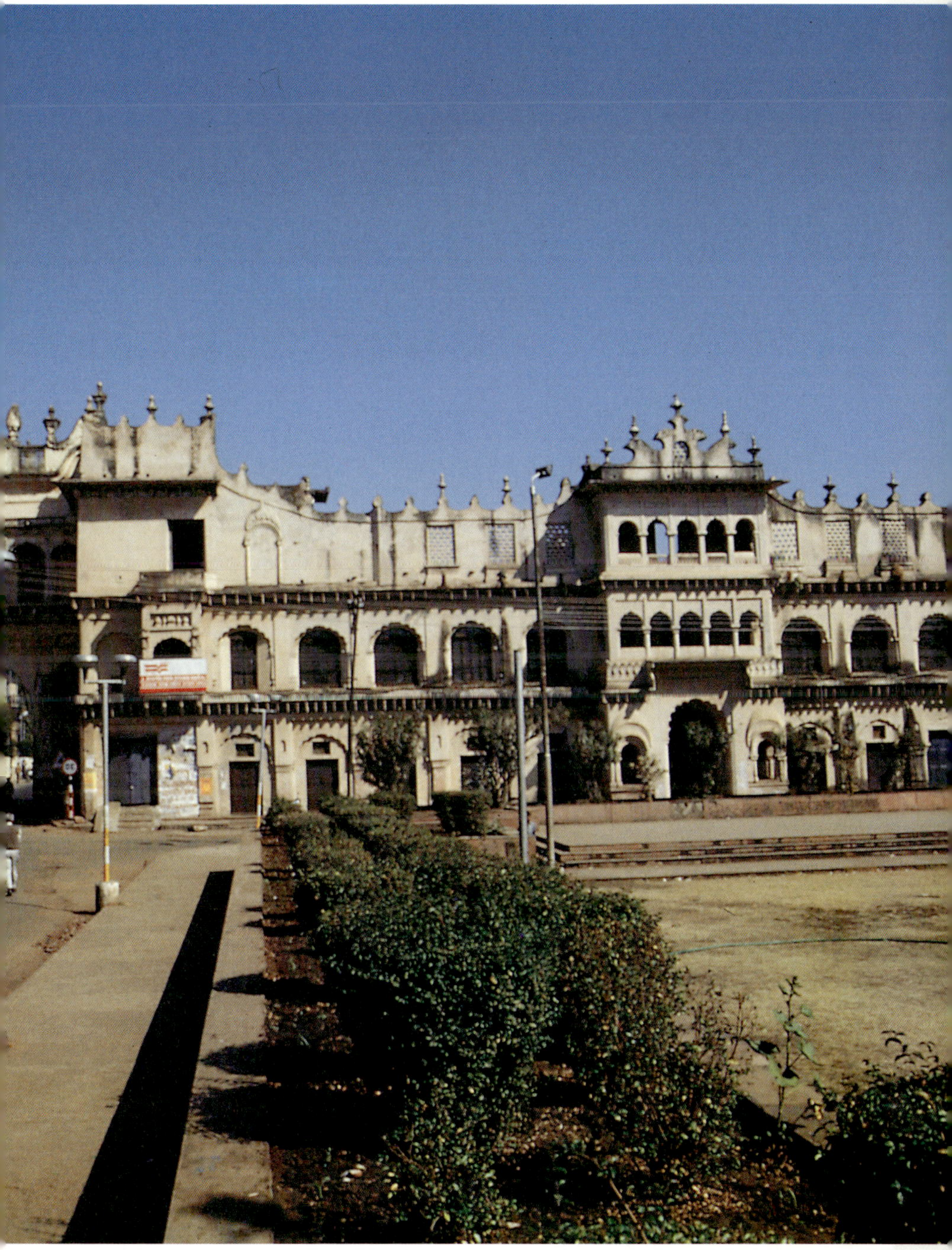

of the architectural wonders of Bhopal and features an exquisite amalgamation of Indo-Islamic as well as European (Italian and French) styles of architecture. The European style emerged due to the presence of the Frenchmen (Bourbons), who occupied influential positions in the court of the nawab begums. A combination of post-Renaissance and Gothic styles find expression in the construction of the charming Shaukat Mahal. Obviously, the mixed style of architecture is quite different from the other interesting architectural specimens existing in Bhopal. Made of white alabaster, the palace features a series of rather complicated triangular-shaped arches on the ceiling. The exterior walls too are adorned with delicate floral patterns. The brick-red large building of Sadar Manzil adjoining the palace once served as the hall of public audience for the ruling nawab begums of Bhopal who resided in Shaukat Mahal. According to the Indian National Trust for Art and Cultural Heritage (INTACH), the palace Shaukat Mahal was the first in the country for which artists from Italy had been specially commissioned for painting decorative frescoes on the wall. Similar artistry is seen within the adjacent palace Sadar Manzil too though it was built much later, in 1884; initially it served as the administrative wing of the Shaukat Mahal, though presently it houses the main office of the Bhopal Municipal Corporation. The two palaces are located facing the Khirniwala

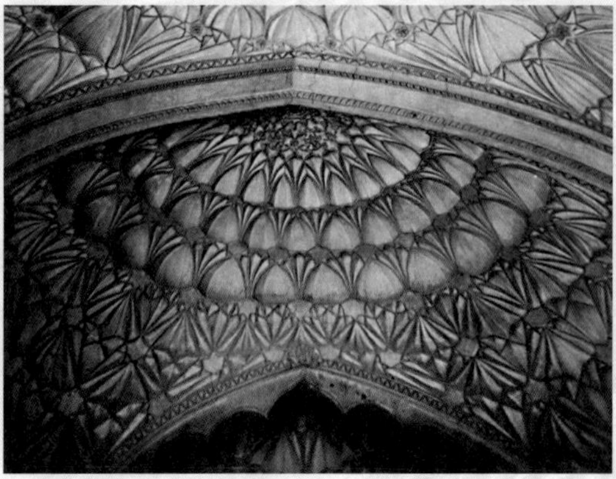

Interior of Shaukat Mahal

Maidan—now renamed as Iqbal Maidan. Several other palatial mansions like the Sheesh Mahal, Zeenat Mahal and Sultan Mahal also lie within the complex. All the palaces around the Iqbal Maidan were once replete with ceiling carvings, coloured-glass decorations, stucco works, wood carvings and Italian style frescoes.

However, older than the Shaukat Mahal is another elegant palace, the Gohar Mahal built in magnificent fusion of Hindu (Gond) and Islamic architecture. The palace, located near the Lower Lake is also known as Nazar Bagh. It was built by Nawab Nazar Mohammad for his wife Qudsia Begum, also called Gohar Ara, who succeeded as

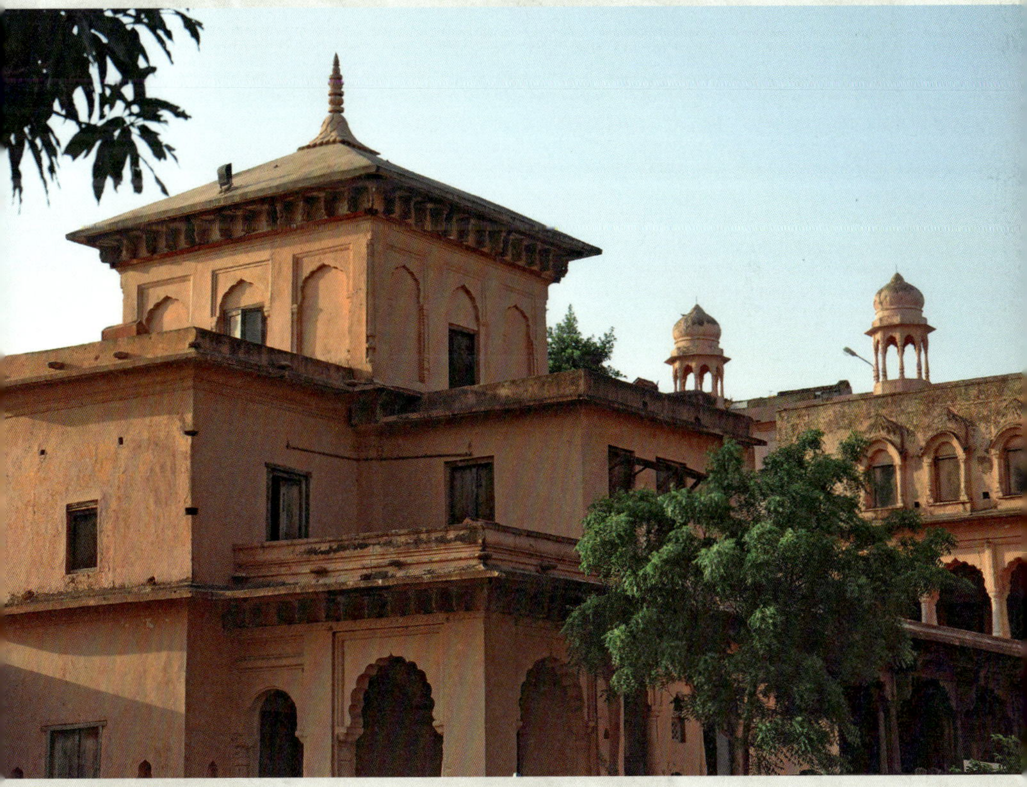

Gohar Mahal

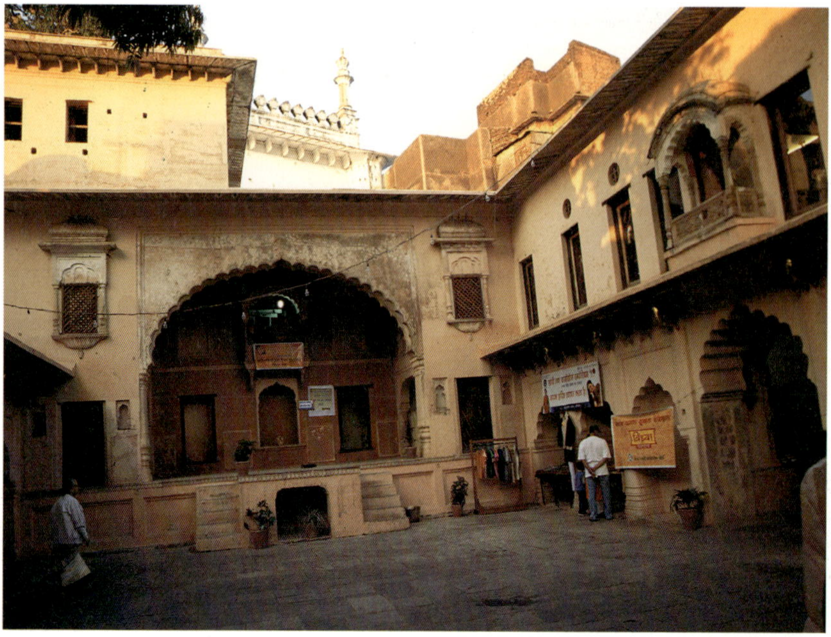

Gohar Mahal Palace, now a venue for craft exhibitions

nawab after the death of her husband. Initially the palace had three courtyards of which just two now remain. The entrance was through a single, though high enough, gateway; on its top were positioned the *choubdars* (drum beaters) who would announce the entry and exit of the nawabs. Gohar Mahal having been renovated, now serves as a popular venue for organising arts and crafts exhibitions attracting artisans from all quarters of the country as well as visitors and customers.

Several other charming mansions were raised by the nawab begums in different parts of the old city of which the most magnificent is known as the Taj Mahal of Bhopal. This extraordinary palace complex was built by Nawab Shah Jahan Begum within her mini-city of Shahjahanabad, depleting the coffers by a sum of thirty lakh

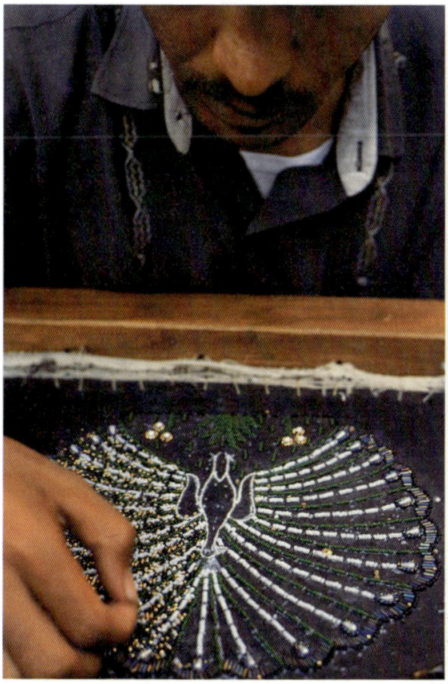

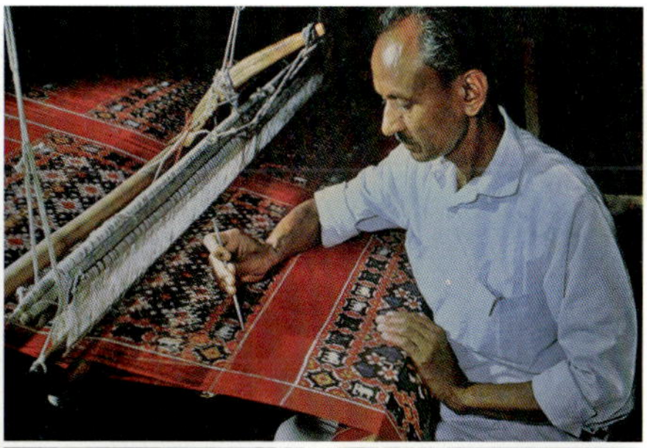

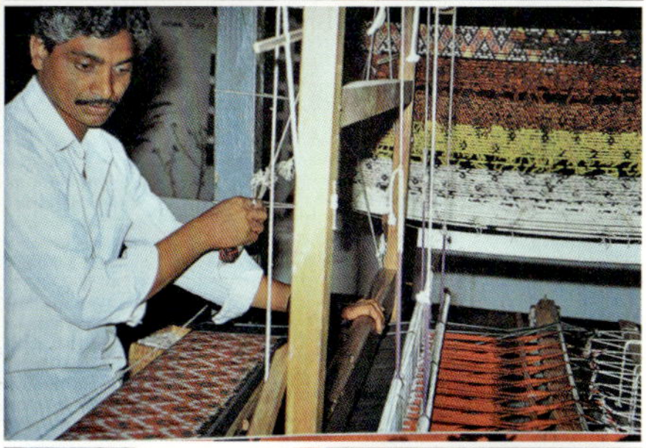

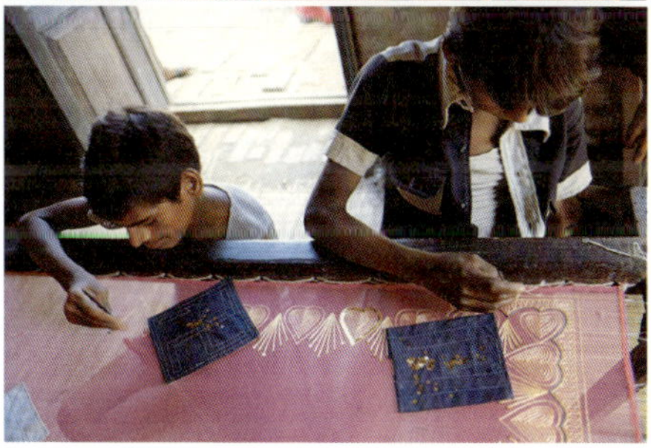

Glass beaded embroidery work displayed by an artisan at an exhibition held at Gohar Mahal (above); a weaver demonstrating his work at an exhibition held at Gohar Mahal (above right); a weaver at Gohar Mahal demonstrating his artwork (right centre); zardozi weavers at an exhibition at Gohar Mahal (right below)

rupees and taking almost 13 years, right from 1871 till 1884, for the completion of construction. It was one of the largest palaces built in the world at that time.

Shah Jahan Begum had initially named this grand building as Raj Mahal (Royal Palace). But the then British Political Resident of Bhopal, highly impressed with its imposing size and striking architecture suggested the name Taj Mahal, comparing it with the world-famous Taj at Agra that was built by the Begum's name-sake, the Mughal

Emperor Shah Jahan. The suggestion was accepted and the palace had been renamed accordingly. It is said that after the completion of the palace the overjoyous Begum had planned a grand inauguration of the palace—"Jashn-e-Taj Mahal"—that lasted for three long years!

The Taj Mahal complex has a fusion of several architectural styles though the predominant stylistic influence being largely Indo-Saracenic. It contains 120 rooms—a Sheesh Mahal (Hall of Mirrors), the Sawan and Bhadon pavilions with fountains simulating the effect of monsoon rains—several courtyards, large halls and long, wide passages. The main entrance is a seven-storey structure. The grand palace was a part of a complex of many buildings built along the lakes that included the Benazir Palace, the Begum's summer resort. The palaces were so oriented that they all enjoyed wafts of cool breeze blowing from the direction of the lakes.

After Partition in 1947, there was an influx of refugees migrating from Pakistan. Nawab Hamidullah Khan allowed the Sindhi refugees to take shelter in the spacious Taj Mahal palace complex, who stayed there for four years until their colony, Sant Hidaram Nagar, was built up at Bairagarh on the outskirts of the city. The Taj Mahal complex had suffered enough damages during this period. Although some members of the royal family too had been living in the same

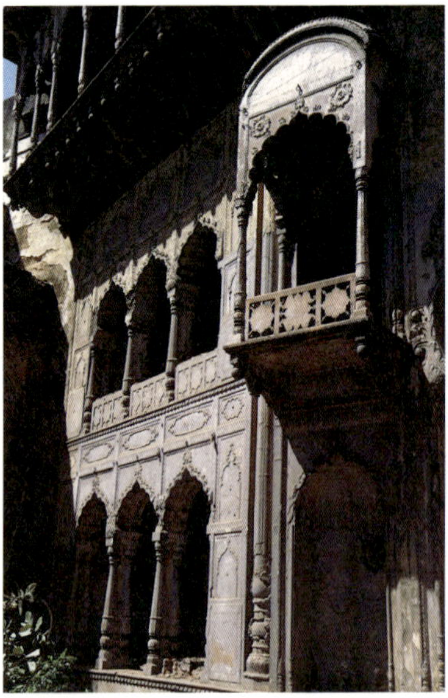

A protruding balcony, Taj Mahal Palace

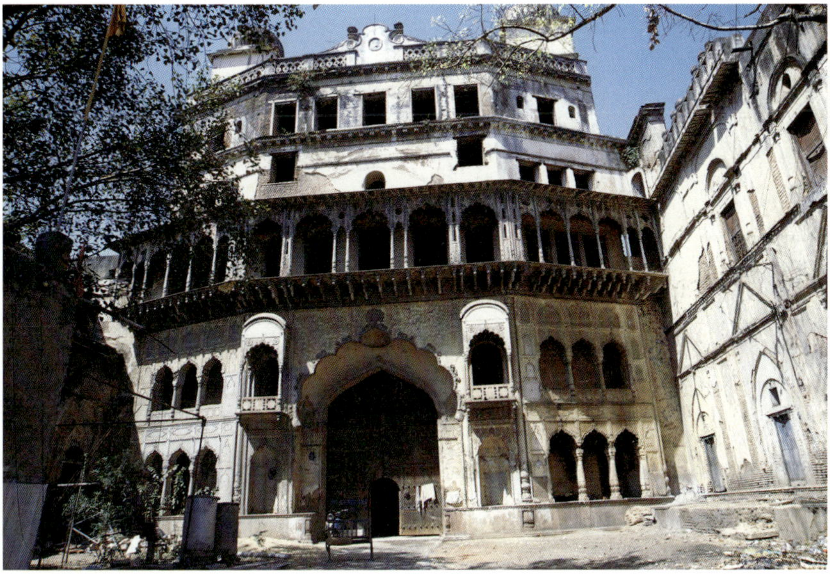

Taj Mahal Palace

palace, unable to meet the cost of repairs and maintenance of the buildings they also moved out gradually. Thus the once-glamorous Taj Mahal was left deserted to its fate for many years, and by 2008 large portions of the palatial edifice had collapsed. Ultimately, the Madhya Pradesh government handed over its charge to the state archaeology department who could only partially restore the damages. A proposal has since been made for converting the Taj Mahal palace into a heritage hotel after necessary renovations.

Of the other palatial buildings constructed in Bhopal during the 20th century the most stunning is the Minto Hall. Its foundation had been laid in November 1909 by Lord and Lady Minto to commemorate their visit to Bhopal, then a princely state in British India. But it was only in 1921 that Nawab Sultan Jahan Begum could finally complete the construction of the palace that was built primarily to be used as the royal guest house close to the Lal Kothi (Raj Bhavan). The architecture of Minto Hall was planned to resemble the decorative crown worn by George V, the British Emperor. The palace contained a spacious hall with highly polished floor where Abida Sultan, then the heir apparent to the royal throne of Bhopal, used to play a new and fast game of roller skates hockey which was her own invention. Later Minto Hall became home to the Hamidia College till the institution shifted elsewhere. After the creation of the state of Madhya Pradesh, Minto Hall served as the Vidhan Sabha of the new state for 40 years from 1956 till 1996.

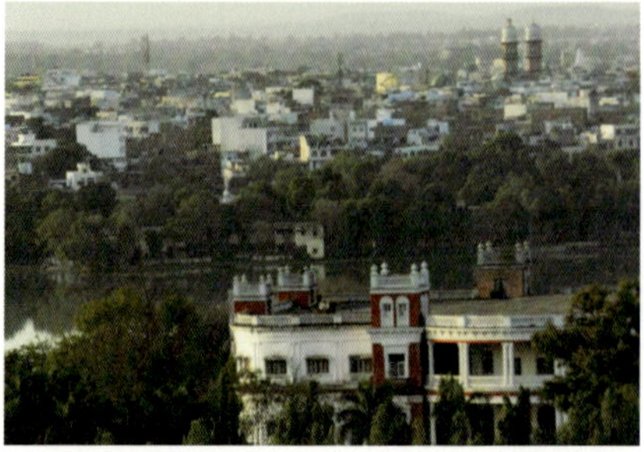

Minto Hall on Lower Lake

The last among the notable constructions that was undertaken by the nawab begums of Bhopal is the Ahmedabad Palace which came up in the 20th century. Built by Nawab Sultan Jahan Begum in the memory of her husband Ahmed Ali Khan, this palace was originally called Qasr-e-Sultani. The edifice is a rectangular double-storey structure; it was the first-ever structure in Bhopal to be built with reinforced concrete bricks, Italian marbles and having installations for electricity connection as well as a water supply pump. As per the Muslim tradition, the palace had separate wings for men and women (zenana). The building has circular pillars, porticos and entrance vestibules; the frescoes in the durbar hall are now a reminder of its glorious past. The Flag Staff House and the Aaina Mahal were further extensions of the palace meant for the royal guests. In one of the wings called Rahat Manzil stayed Mahatma Gandhi when he came to Bhopal in 1929. Ahmedabad Palace is also the birth place of Bhopal's last titular Nawab, Tiger Mansoor Ali Khan Pataudi. The palace is today home to the Saifia College, an old reputed academic institution of Bhopal. Another palace Noor-us-Sabah has now been converted into a prestigious heritage hotel.

Ancient Heritage Sites

Other than the architectural achievements of the nawabs, Bhopal also has several world-renowned ancient heritage sites in its periphery. Barely 20 km south of the BHEL domain lies the ancient township of Bhojpur that was founded by the Paramara king Bhoj in the early 11th century; the vast lake Sagar Tal being one of his creations. The lake exists no more, having been destroyed long ago by Sultan Hoshang Shah, but what survives today is the stupendous shrine dedicated to lord Bhojeshwara or Shiva that was raised on what was earlier its bank. Though never

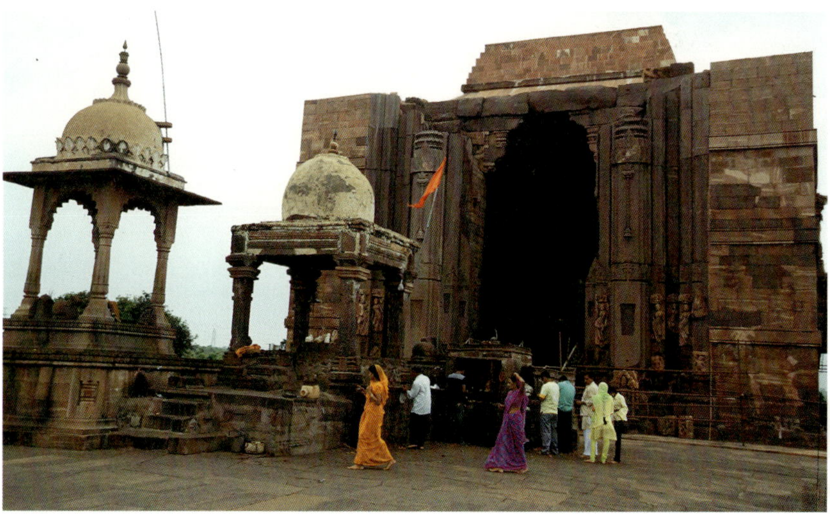

Bhojeshwara Temple in Bhojpur, founded by Raja Bhoj

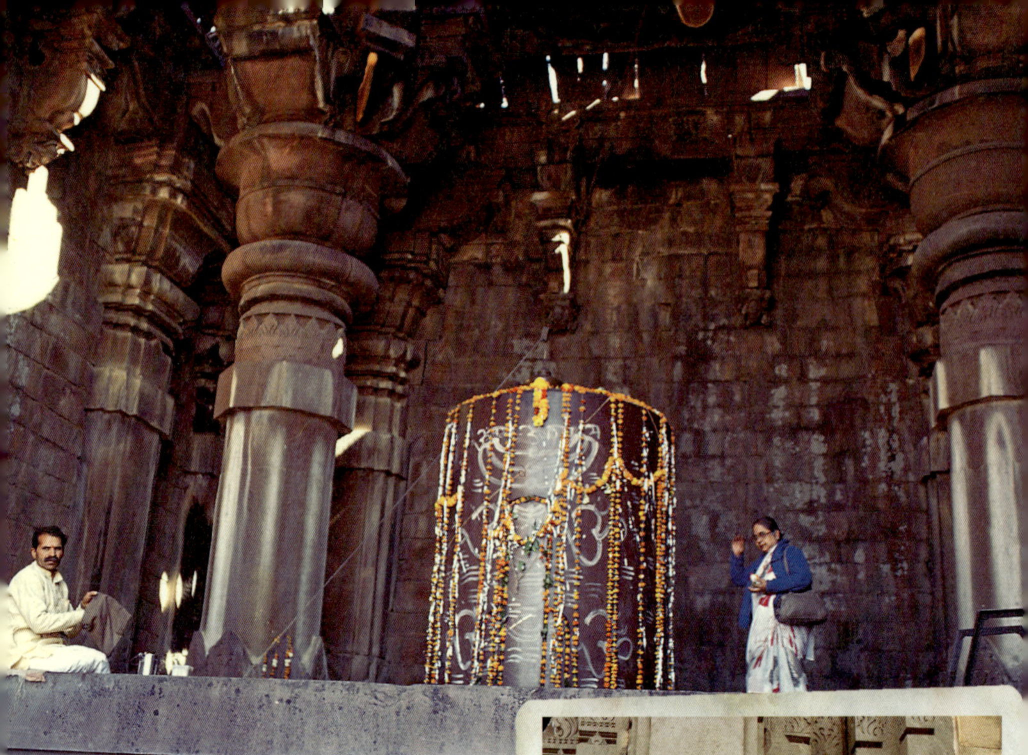

The 8-foot-high Shiva lingam, Bhojeshwara Temple, Bhojpur

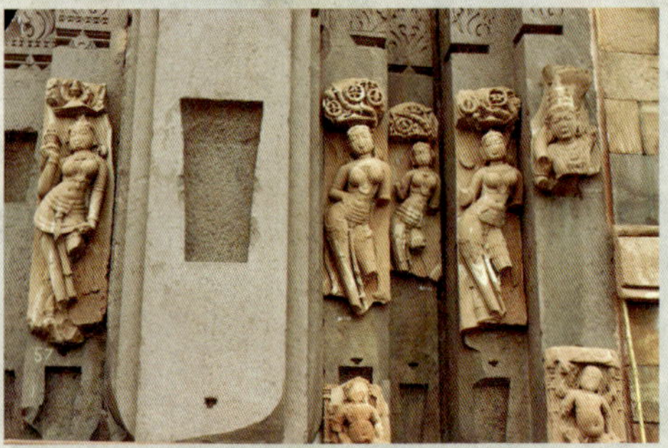

Exquisite sculpture on the facade of the Bhojeshwara Temple

completed, the 80-foot-high temple stands erect till this day in all its architectural grandeur. With its facade adorned with some superb sculptures of celestial figures, the huge sandstone temple originally overlooked the vast lake. Today the shrine stands on a rocky plane or rampart which is 17 feet higher than the surrounding ground level while the temple base occupies an area of 120 x 77 sq. ft. From an architectural point of view, the shrine is of unconventional design without having any covering roof on top. According to myths and local belief, building this mammoth temple was no ordinary man's job; it was supposedly constructed by the all-powerful Pandavas

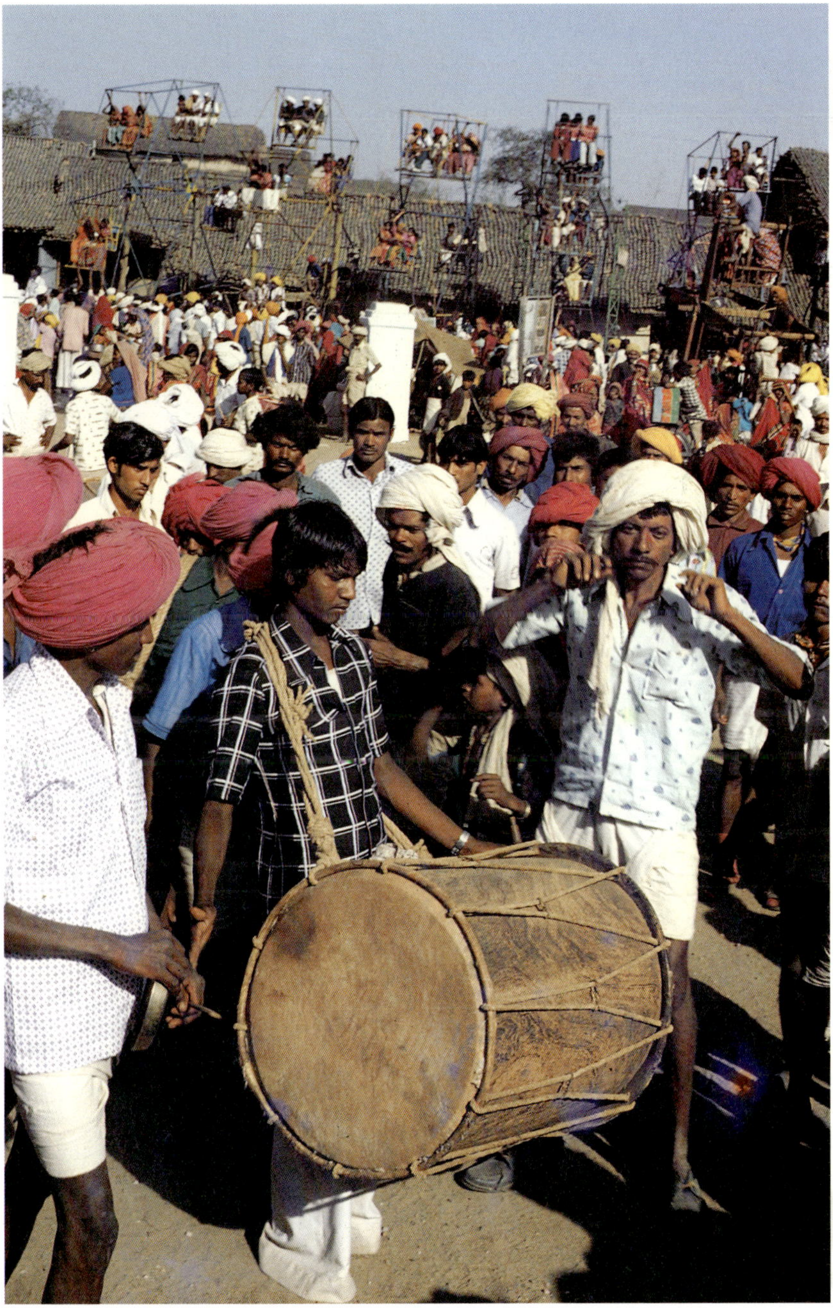

Village fair during Shivratri festival, Bhojpur

during the period of their life that passed in exile. Inside the temple is enshrined lord Shiva in his finely polished lingam image, carved out from a massive single monolith, standing 8 foot high and 18 foot in circumference, and is acclaimed as the world's largest monolithic Shiva!

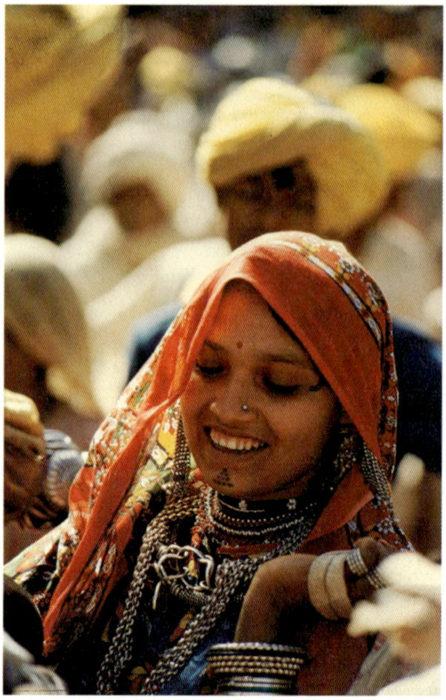

A rural woman all decked up for Shivratri, Bhojpur

Standing in its vicinity is yet another monolithic shrine which belongs to the Jain community; it houses the 20-foot-high colossal monolithic figure of lord Mahavira, which too is one of the largest in the country.

Proceeding further southwards, about 45 km from Bhopal, lies the famous World Heritage Site—Bhimbetka; the term in local dialect means the sitting place or the camping ground of Bhima, the second of the Pandava brothers of the Mahabharata fame. The site remains strangely concealed within the southern fringe of the forest-clad, craggy Vindhya Range. In this rocky terrain of jungles and hidden cliffs, spread over an area of 1,893 hectares, there exists more than 1,000 rock shelters belonging to the ancient cavemen of the Paleolithic age (1,00,000 BC or earlier). There one can see some really wonderful rock art—a profusion of vivid, panoramic paintings in more than 600 caves distributed in five clusters, making it obvious to believe that there were some artists amongst those cave dwellers

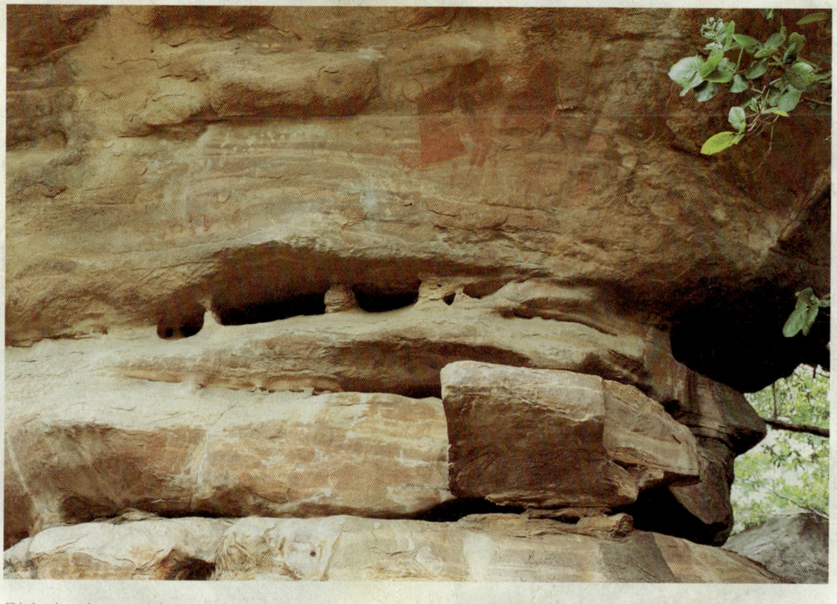

Bhimbetka prehistorical rock shelter and painting

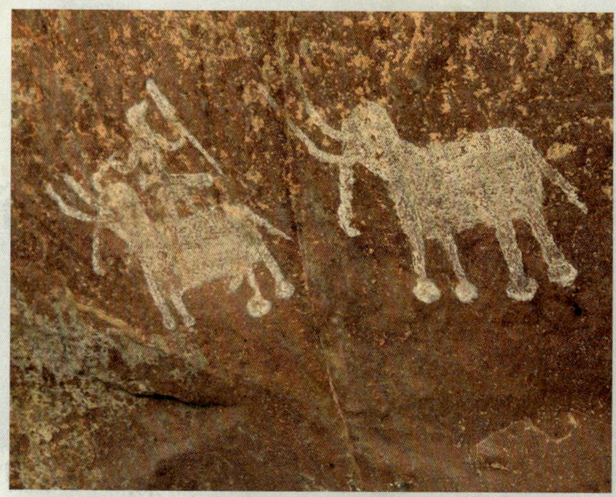

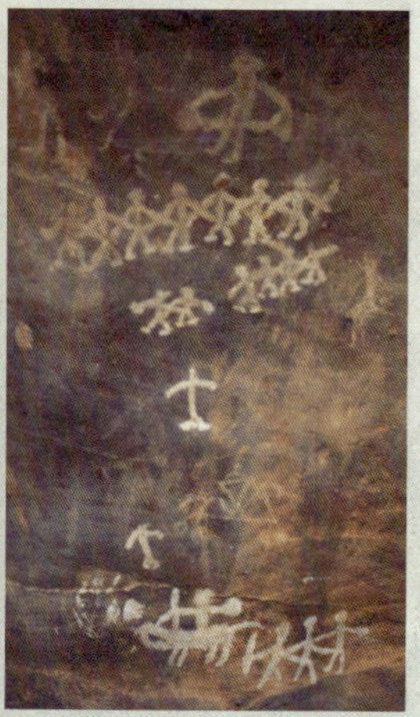

Bhimbetka rock shelter painting depicting animal figures (left); Bhimbetka prehistoric cave painting depicting figures in a group dance (right)

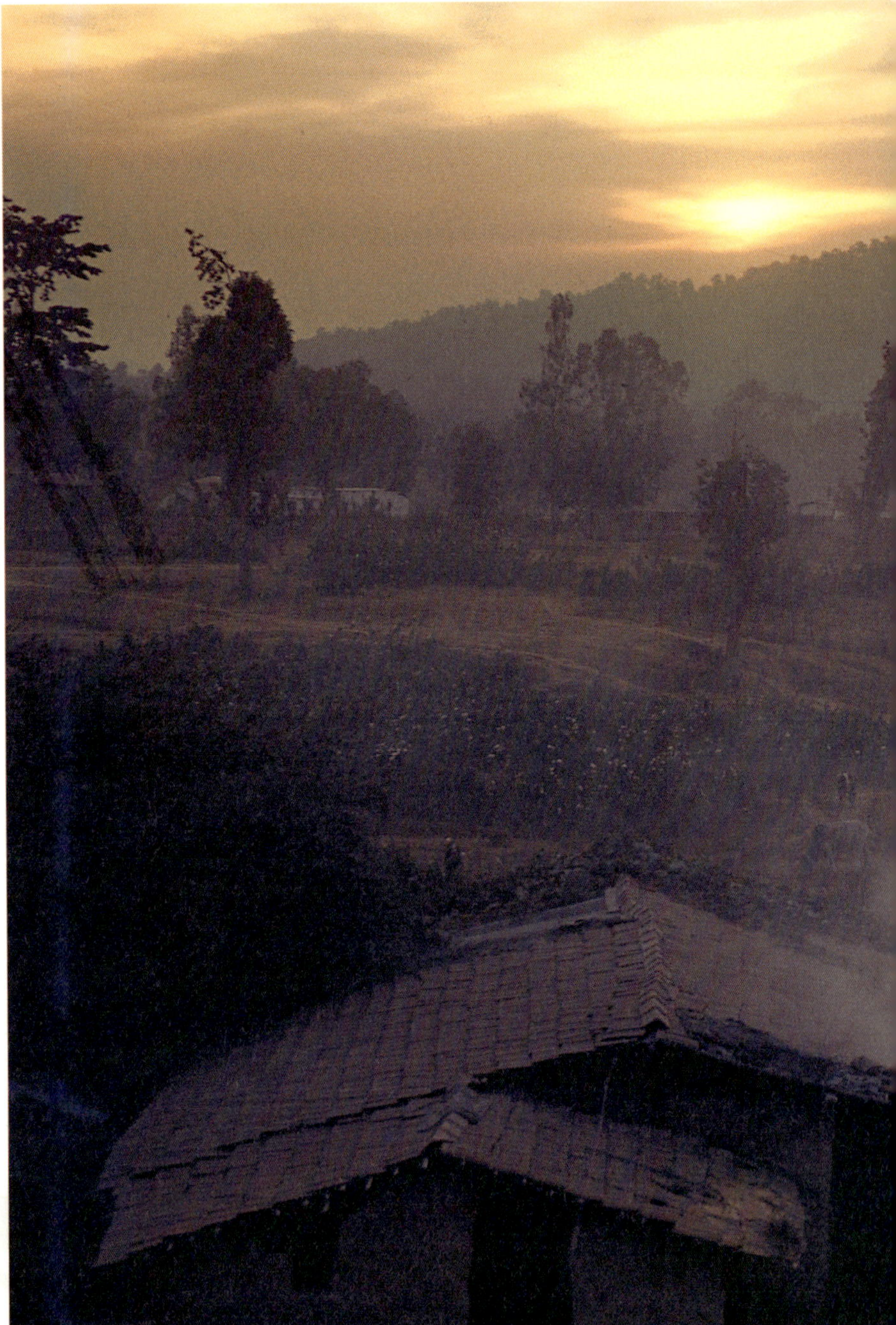

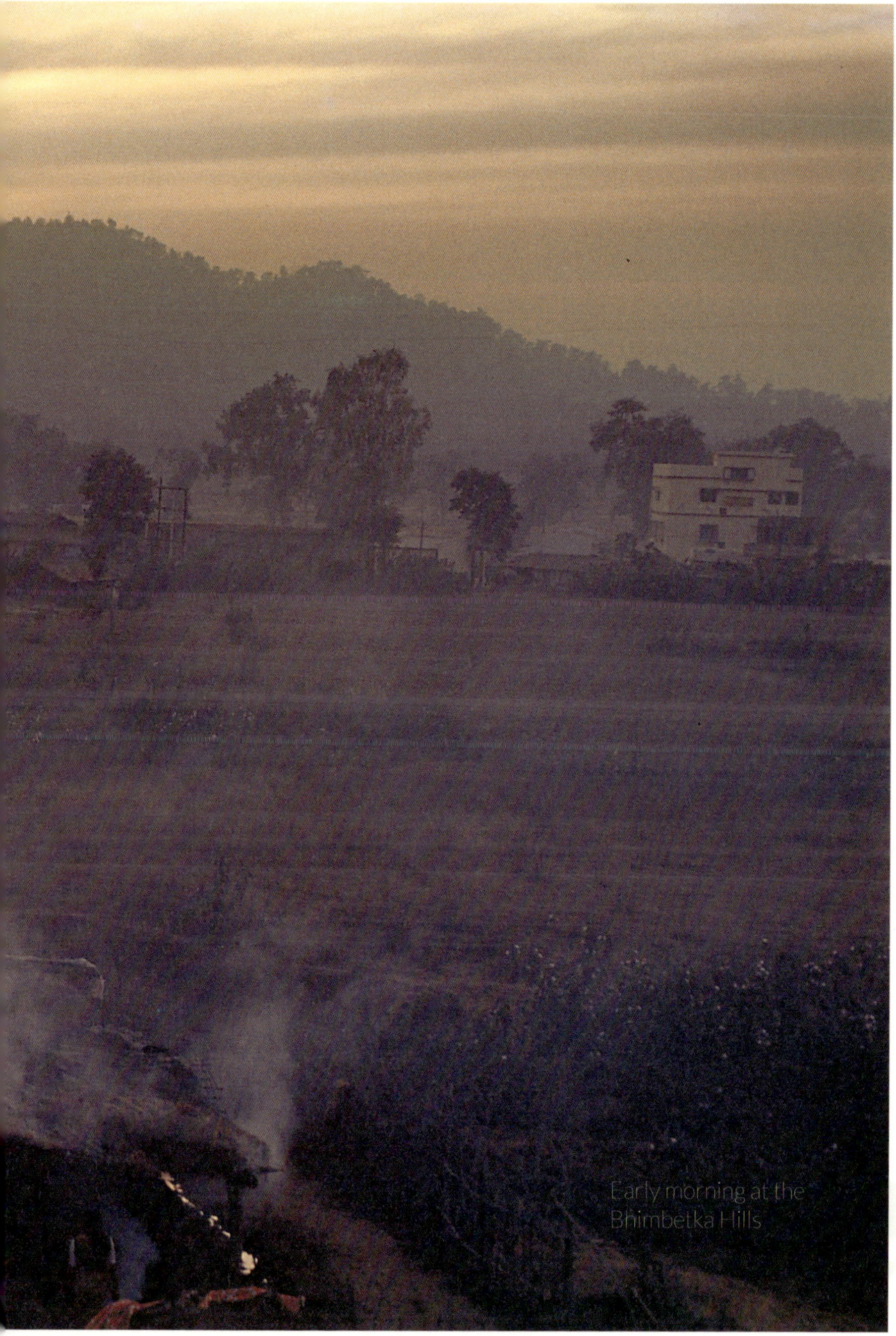
Early morning at the Bhimbetka Hills

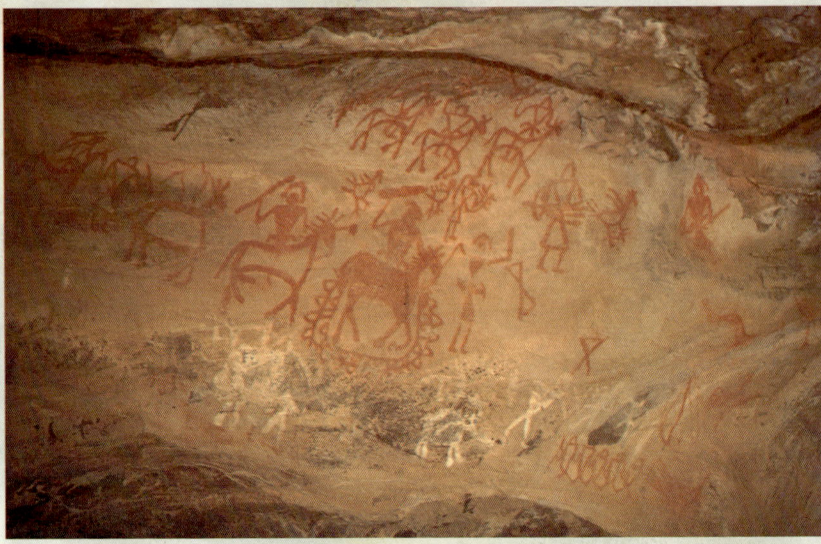

Rock painting depicting warriors going for an expedition, Bhimbetka

who lived during the lower Paleolithic and the Neolithic periods down to the early historic age (from 10,000 BC till more recent). Executed mainly in red and white colour with occasional use of green and yellow, the paintings chiefly depict the various wild animals that were abounding in the region in those days—bisons, tigers, lions, antelopes, elephants and even the rhinoceros. Also painted are scenes of hunting, and the very interesting depictions of the ways of community life of the pre-historic cavemen who lived there thousands of years ago. Like the aboriginal rock paintings of Kakadu National Park in Australia, the Bushmen settlements in Kalahari Desert of Africa, the cave art of Altamira in Spain and the Lascaux cave paintings in France, the rock art site of Bhimbetka group of cave shelters also has been recognised as a rare archaeological treasure trove, an invaluable chronicle in the history of mankind. In the year 2003, UNESCO declared Bhimbetka as a World Heritage

Site for its precious treasure of cave paintings as well as various other pre-historic finds of daily utility implements related to the ancient cave dwellers. The Bhimbetka site was a chance discovery by the celebrated archaeologist Late V.S. Wakankar in the year 1958. Later, several other similar sites, though small and isolated, have also been found in the Shamla Hills, Lalghati and Bhadbhada areas, all located around the city of Bhopal. Such discoveries only go on to corroborate the fact that Bhopal and its surrounding region is located on one of the most ancient sites of settlement on earth.

Few cities in the world can feel as proud as Bhopal for housing two World Heritage Sites within its small ambit or within a radius of just 50 km or even less! Apart from the pre-historic site of Bhimbetka, Bhopal has another great World Heritage treasury—the famous Buddhist shrine at Sanchi, located towards the north-east of the city and barely 46 km away on the main railways taking up only an hour's travel by train. The distance is greater of course, if the journey is undertaken by road. But in that eventuality a visit to the ancient historic fort of Raisen that comes on way, would be more than rewarding.

Built in the early 13th century the Raisen Fort with its strong, high walls and nine imposing gateways had served long as one of the vital centres for administering the Malwa region. Though dilapidated now, this impregnable fort has sheltered various dynasties that ruled Bhopal for over six centuries. Consisting of several palaces, temples, mosques, graves, wells, cannons and a large tank, the deserted citadel is presently worthy of architectural and historic interest only. The Mandu sultanate was in control of the fort since long, but it had changed hands several times. In 1760 this crucial fort was occupied by Nawab Faiz Mohammad Khan of Bhopal when he declared himself as the Mughal *faujdar* of the Raisen pargana. Accommodating the sacred shrines belonging to different religions within its complex, Raisen bears testimony of the communal integration that once prevailed there.

Just 23 km north of Raisen is Sanchi, the oldest and the most magnificent of all Buddhist shrines in the country, which lies on top of a hilly mound called Vidishagiri. Vidishagiri presents the scene of a widely spread out field containing big and small structures of Buddhist stupas and *chaityas* (chortens), rising above the scattered ruins. The main structure, shaped in the form of a large hemisphere or stupa, was originally a brick work; later it had been covered with stone for protection against weathering. The stupa was built by the great Mauryan Emperor Ashoka in the 3rd century BC. Along with its dome and a stone umbrella topping the centre, the structure rises to 16.4 m above ground, while diametrically it measures 37 m. The whole construction is encircled by an ascending narrow pathway fenced with stone railings. The entrance is through the four high and spectacular stone gateways standing at the four cardinal points. The gates are profusely carved all around with intricate decorative imageries. During the later centuries many other smaller stupas had come up on the site as well as in the neighbouring areas. The main stupa and the row of high vertical columns alongside, near the southern gate, are considered to be the oldest stone architecture of India. Enshrined within the main stupa are the sacred mortal remains of the Buddha, while the smaller stupa next to it contains the relics of his two disciples—Sariputta and Maudgalyayana.

As the greatest and most important Buddhist centre in India Sanchi had thrived for about thousand years from the 3rd

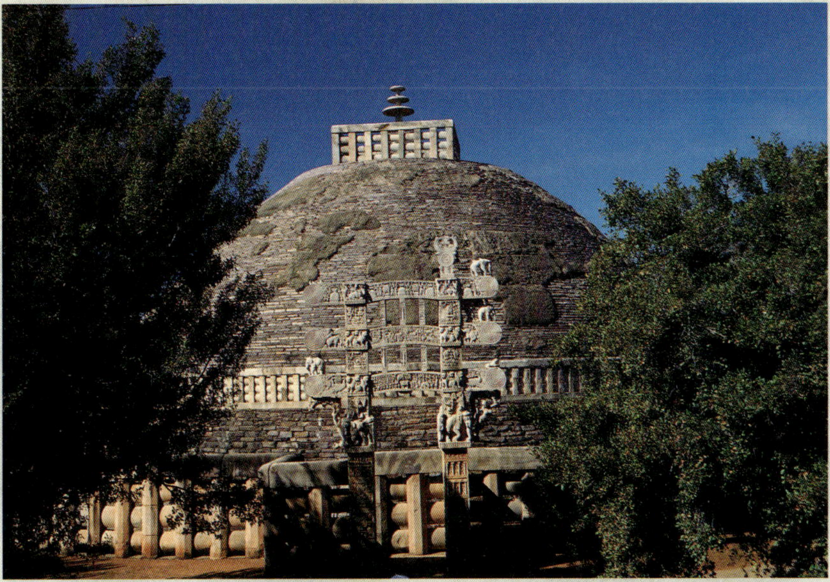

The great stupa of Sanchi, view from the eastern gate

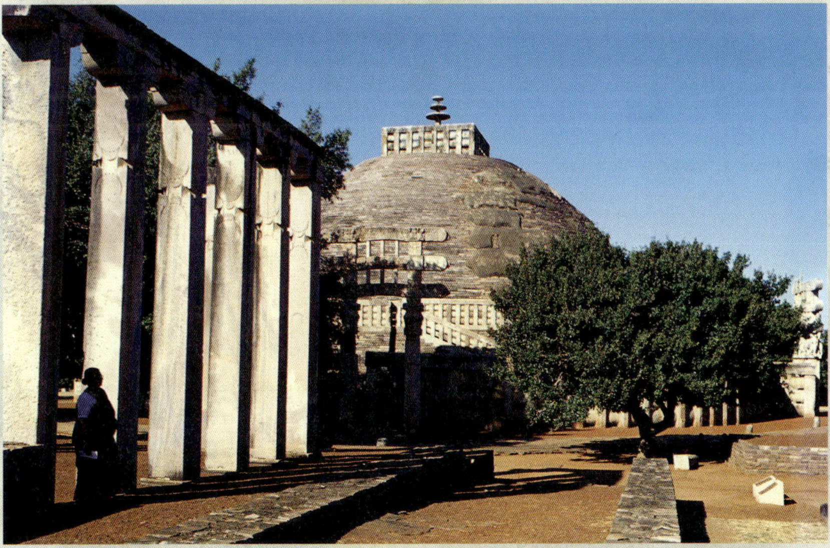

Sanchi

century BC till 7th century AD. After Emperor Ashoka and the later Mauryans there was a revival of Hinduism in the country that subdued the influence of Buddhism considerably; with the passage of time Buddhism had further suffered a decline in India—its own birth place. For being assimilated within the tenets of Hinduism, Buddha was accepted and absorbed as an incarnate of lord Vishnu, the prime Hindu God. The result was that those Buddhist stupas lying on the hill top gradually lost their importance to people who were largely Hindus. Deserted, the shrines lay exposed to the vagaries of nature for years and the once-famous site was ultimately forgotten altogether.

For many centuries the place remained dilapidated, covered under thick deposits of soil on which grew varied vegetations, as a result of which the exquisitely carved gateways had fallen down. It was merely by chance that some British army officer could rediscover the site in the year 1818. But, for still many more years nothing could be done for damage repair and preservation of the world-famous Buddhist shrine; rather, after discovery it had been subjected to wanton destruction by local vandals and treasure hunters. Finally, it was the archaeologist Alexander Cunningham working under Sir John Marshall, Director General of the Archaeological Survey of India (ASI), whose efforts had helped successfully salvage the damaged structures and restore them to their present glory. The expenses of revival and restoration work of this ancient Buddhist shrine was largely funded by Sultan Jahan Begum, the last female ruling Nawab of Bhopal at the insistence of Cunningham. It is a rare example of the thoughtful permissiveness of an Islamic state allowing other religions to survive and flourish under its tutelage.

Today as we find them, the four magnificent *toranas* or gateways of the main stupa are all replete with exquisite carvings presenting scenes from the tales of the *Jatakas* or the life stories of the Buddha in his previous births. Though never seen in the depictions, Buddha's very presence is indicated through various symbols—the lotus representing his birth, the tree his enlightenment, the wheel representing his sermon while the footprints and throne symbolising his presence. The delicate and exquisitely stone-carved figures of men, animals, dwarfs and *yakshis*—all full of subtle humane expressions, have so dexterously been chiselled out that many archaeologists believe that their sculptors possibly belonged to the communities of the skilled artisans like the ivory carvers and precision art-jewellers for which the nearby region of Vidisha was once famous.

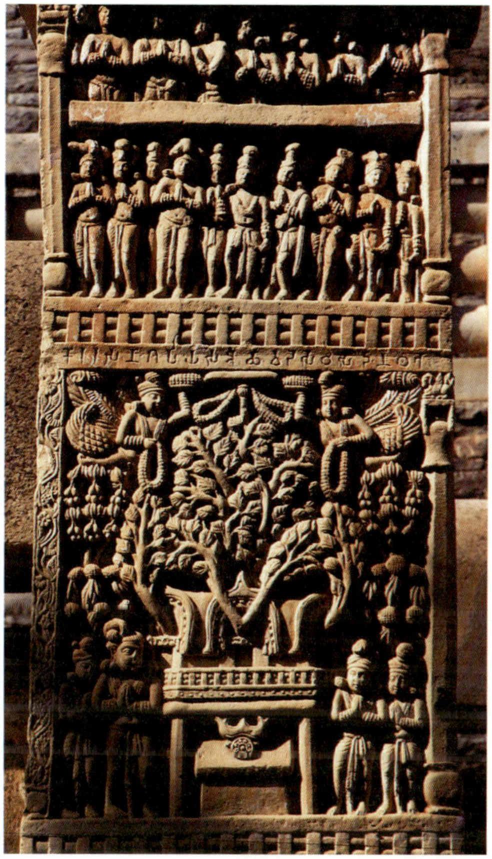

Scenes from the *Jataka Tales* etched on the facade of the gate, Sanchi

The surviving portion of the finely executed base of one of the broken stone pillars erected by Ashoka, stands close to the

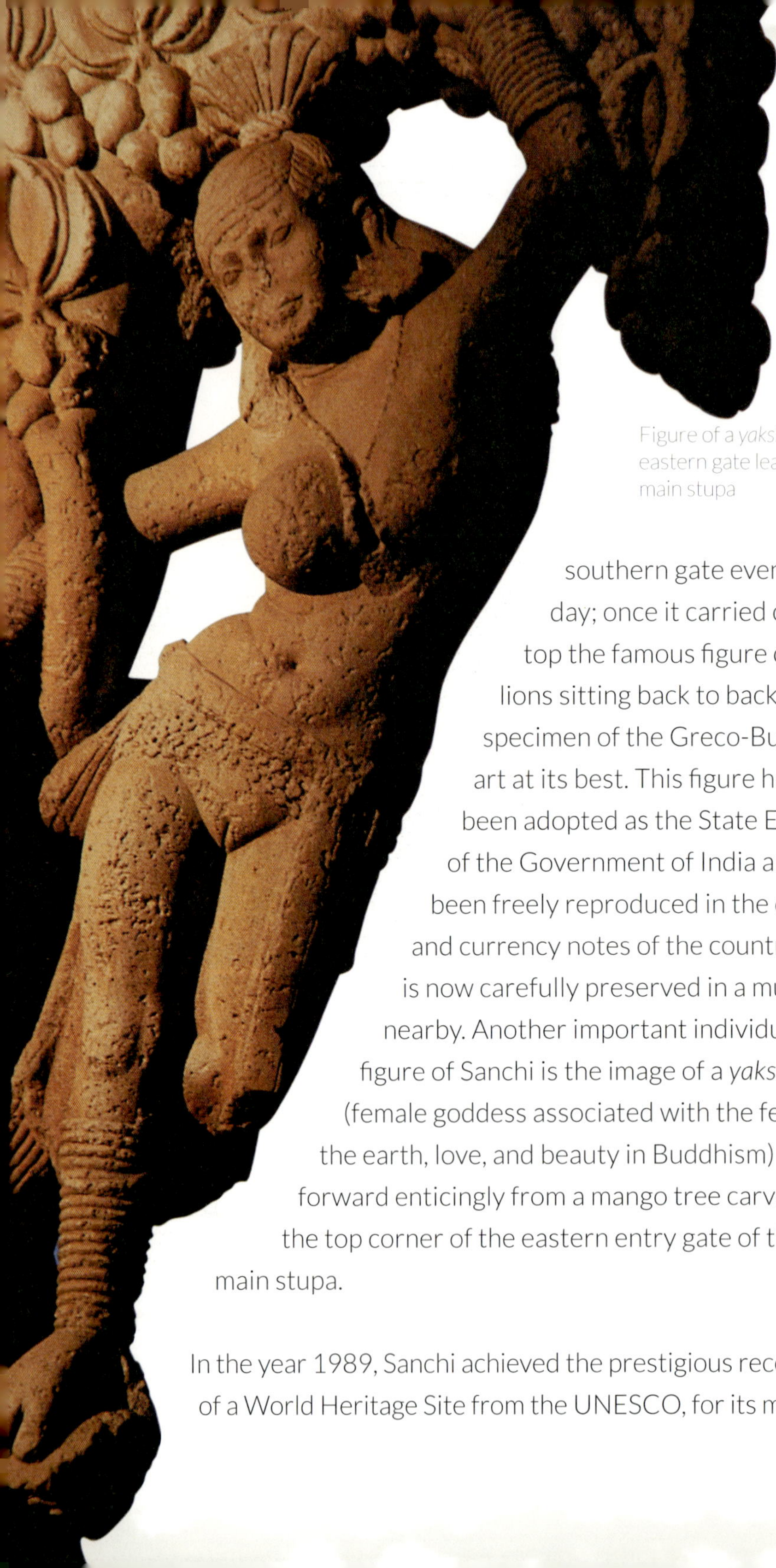

Figure of a *yakshi* on the eastern gate leading to the main stupa

southern gate even to this day; once it carried on its top the famous figure of three lions sitting back to back—a fine specimen of the Greco-Buddhist art at its best. This figure has since been adopted as the State Emblem of the Government of India and has been freely reproduced in the coins and currency notes of the country. It is now carefully preserved in a museum nearby. Another important individual figure of Sanchi is the image of a *yakshi* (female goddess associated with the fertility of the earth, love, and beauty in Buddhism) leaning forward enticingly from a mango tree carved on the top corner of the eastern entry gate of the main stupa.

In the year 1989, Sanchi achieved the prestigious recognition of a World Heritage Site from the UNESCO, for its more than 2,000-year-old precious treasure trove of India's sculptural art heritage related to Buddhism.

Wandering through the ruins scattered all around the stupa complex, or lazing in the peaceful surroundings near the figure of the meditating Buddha in the niche of the main stupa, one feels as if the wisdom and compassion of Emperor Ashoka still lingers amidst the peaceful surroundings at Sanchi—not too far away from the city of Bhopal!

Wondrous Mosques

Being the second largest Muslim-ruled state in the country after Hyderabad, Bhopal is inevitably replete with Islamic shrines including mosques of varied dimensions and magnificence. Of the three important mosques in the city, the oldest is the Jama Masjid which was built by the first woman ruler of the state, Nawab Qudsia Begum. Though constructed as early as 1837, it still retains its old charisma impressing the visitors with its imposing grandeur. Its two lofty minarets can be sighted from a distance. The Masjid has three large bulbous domes, though more attractive is the ornate interior which is a fine example of Islamic architecture perfected with white

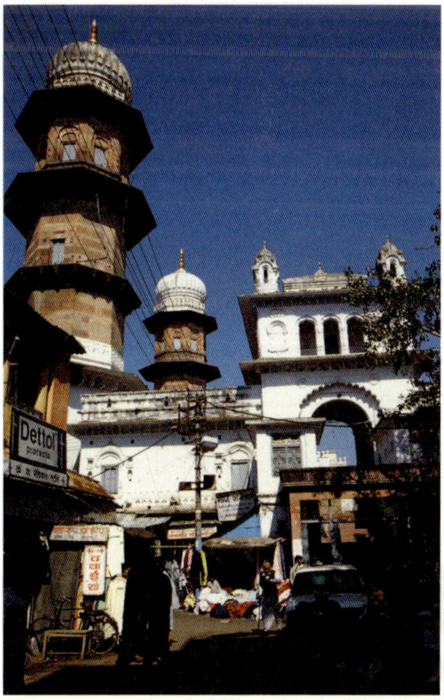

Jama Masjid in Chowk Bazar

alabaster-columned arches while the inner sanctum is built in all marble. There is a large pond in the vast courtyard outside. Much of the view of the grand Jama Masjid lie obscured by the congested area of Chowk Bazar that has gradually sprung up around this grand edifice.

The elegant Moti Masjid or Pearl Mosque is another fine landmark of Bhopal. Modelled on the Jama Masjid of Delhi it is located at the city centre and was constructed

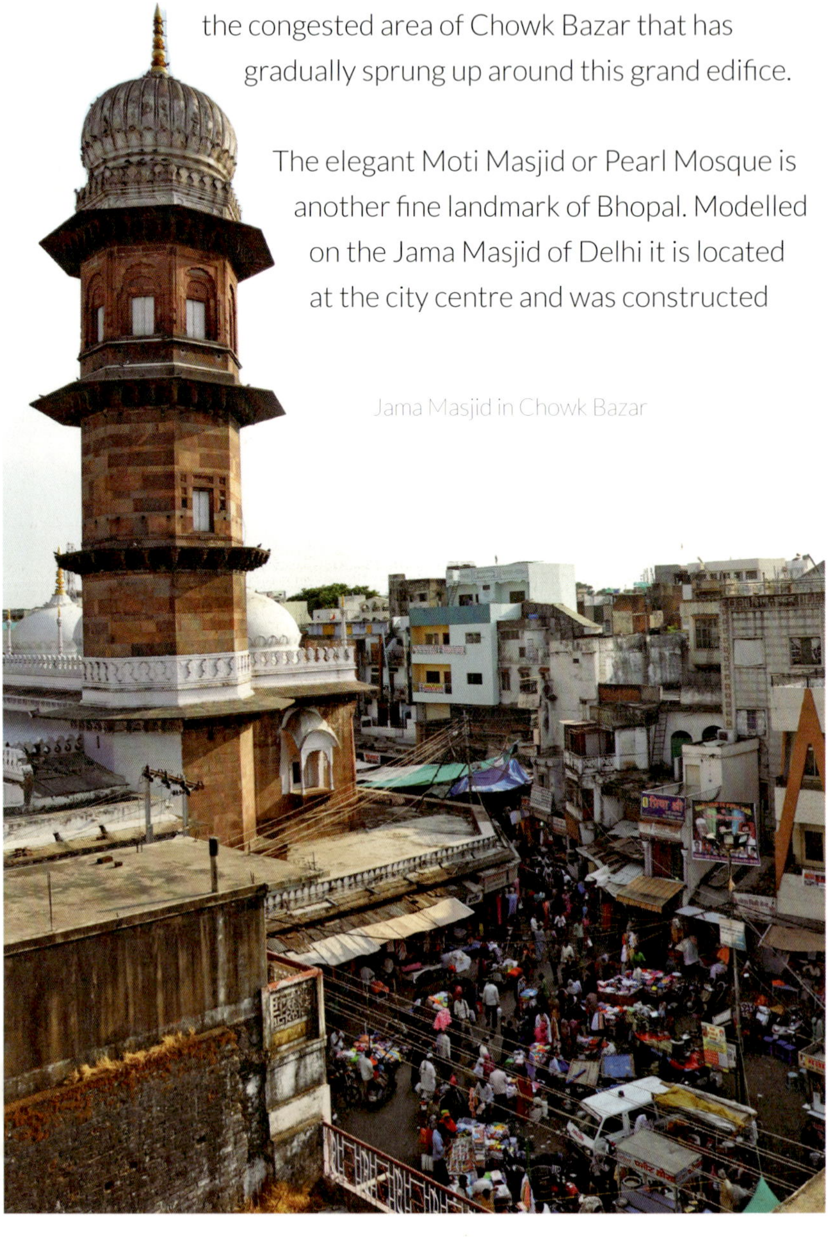

Jama Masjid in Chowk Bazar

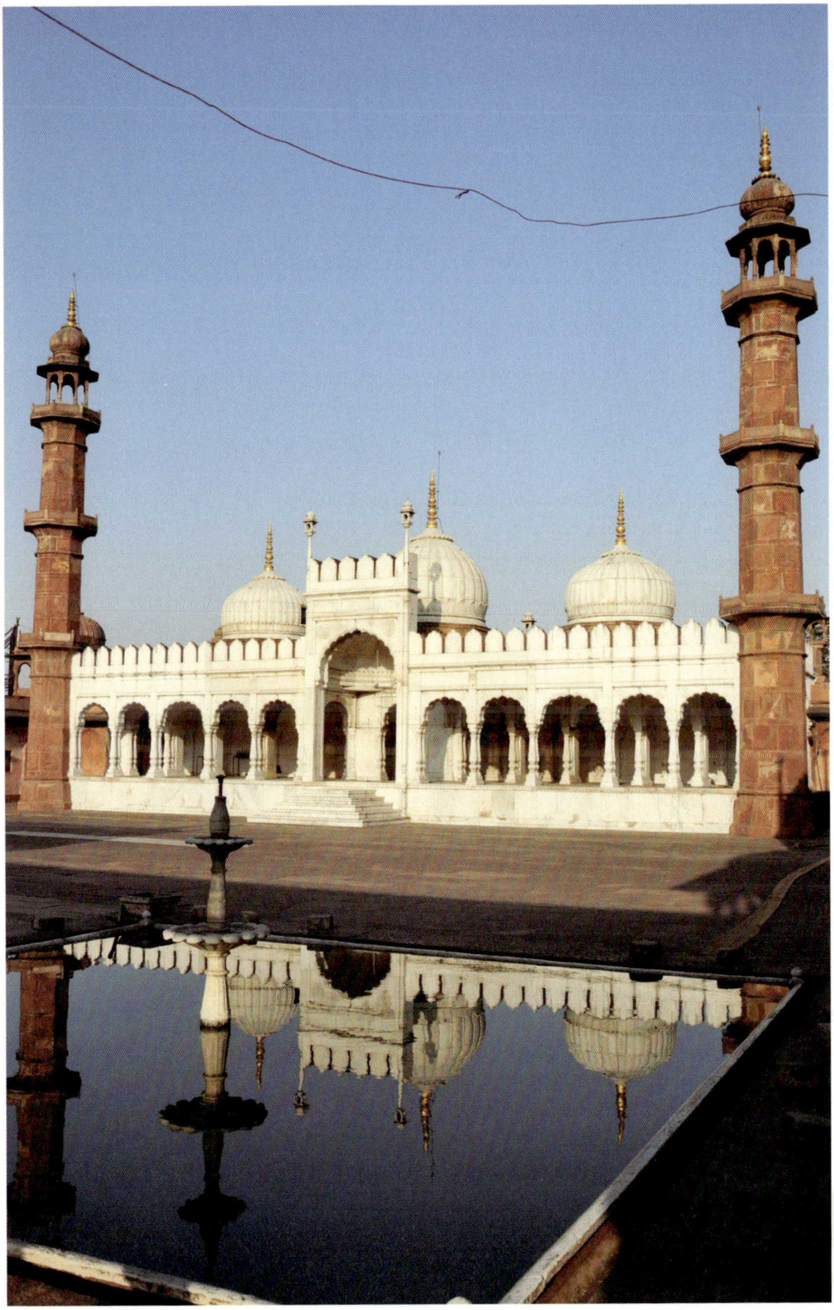

Moti Masjid

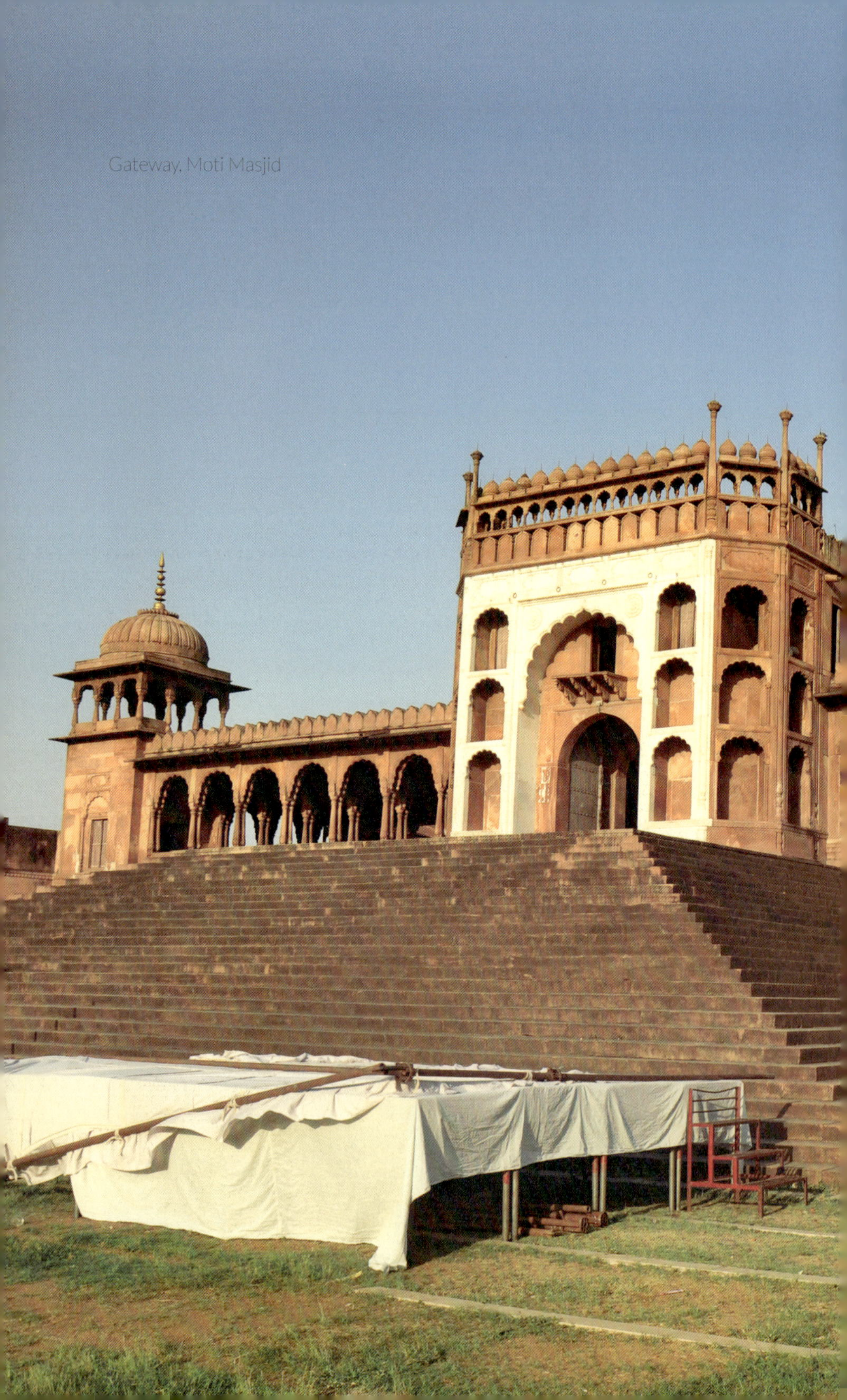

Gateway, Moti Masjid

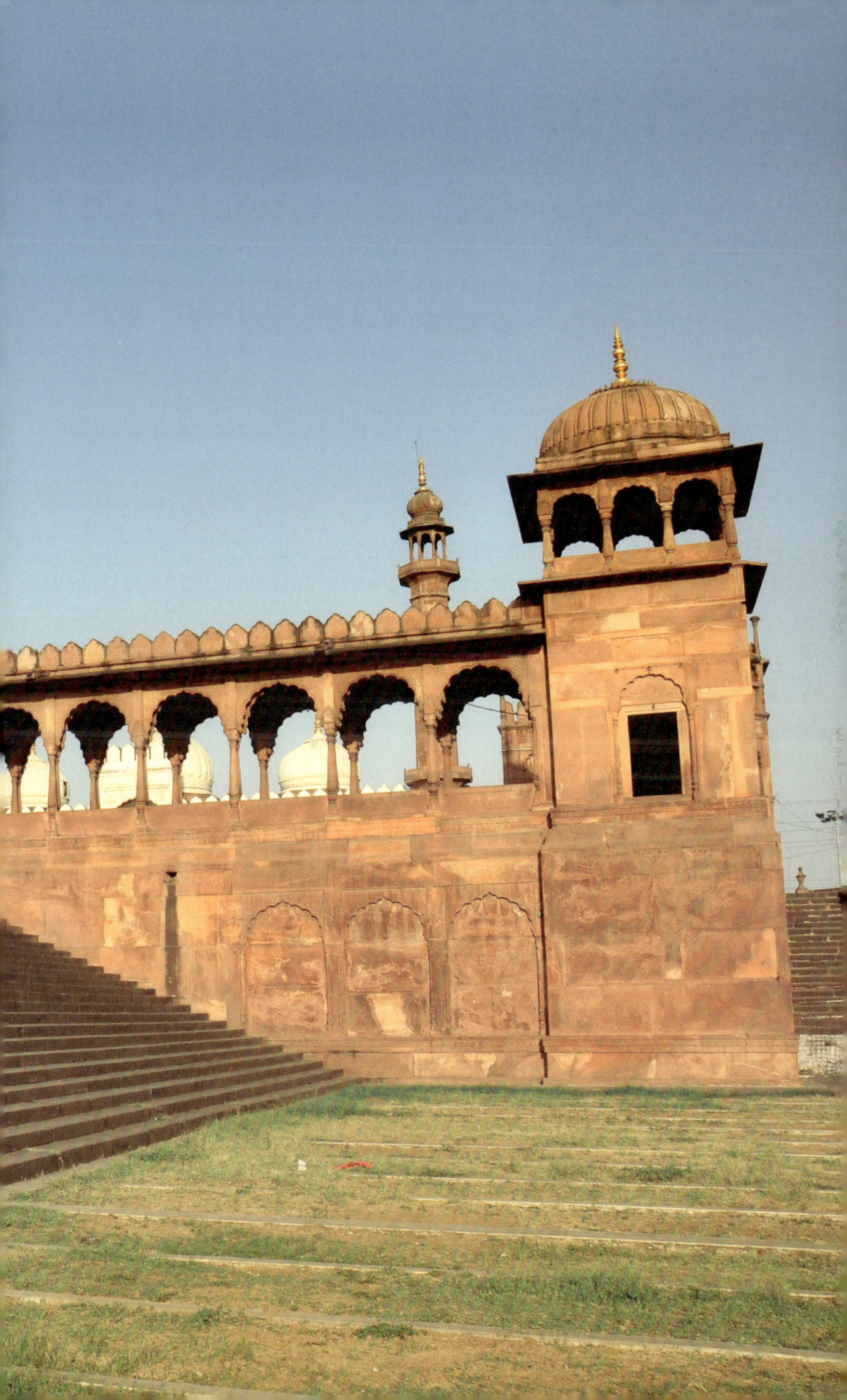

by Nawab Sikandar Jahan Begum, daughter of Qudsia Begum, in the year 1860. A neatly built structure, Moti Masjid boasts of its all-white marble facade. Preserved well over the years, it has a nice modern look with two marble cupolas and two dark red minarets on either side which are further adorned with bright golden spikes on top.

However, the pride of the place in Bhopal goes to Taj-ul-Masajid, the grandest of all magnificent landmarks in the capital. Constructed over an area of 7,065 sq. m it is the world's third largest mosque according to the Archaeological Survey of India. The large edifice is capable of accommodating over a lakh of devotees at a time. The name Taj-ul-Masajid, literally meaning the "Crown of Mosques" is well justified. The massive structure has a pink facade topped by two 62-m high octagonal minarets with marble domes. Like sentinels they guard the three bulbous principal domes from either side. The interior of the mosque has an impressive hallway with attractive pillars and marble flooring similar to the Jama Masjid of Delhi or the stupendous Badshahi Mosque of Lahore. The lofty main entrance is a 24-m high double storey opening with four archways and nine-cusped manifold openings leading to the the main prayer hall. Eleven arches allow entrance into the vast prayer hall with all supporting pillars intricately designed, while the internal northern part is reserved for the veiled women for performing namaz.

Construction of Taj-ul-Masajid was initiated by Nawab Sultan Jahan Begum in 1877, who wanted to bring to Bhopal the honour of possessing a mosque of unsurpassed grandeur. But she could not complete its construction during her lifetime for the lack of funds. After a long layoff for about 100 years, its construction was resumed in 1971. As a result of the great efforts of two pious noblemen—Allama Mohammad Imran Khan and Maulana Sayed Hashmat Ali, the great mosque was finally completed in 1985. The eastern gate was renovated grandly using ancient motifs from Syrian mosques (Circa 1250) by the contribution of the Emir of Kuwait wishing to commemorate his departed wife.

With a large pond within its extensive courtyard and the Motia Talab (Lake) on the boundary, the Taj-ul-Masajid is an ever-imposing, unparalleled heritage site of Bhopal. Besides being a centre of worship the mosque is also used as a madrasa or school for Islamic religious studies. Until recent years, it was the congregation site for people coming from all over the country and abroad to attend the three-day-long celebration of Ijtima.

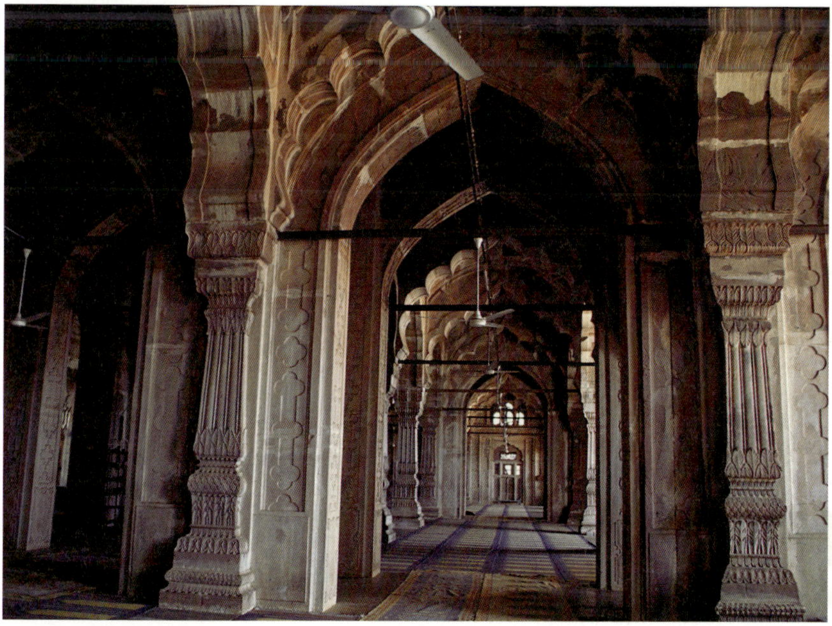

Interior, Taj-ul-Masajid

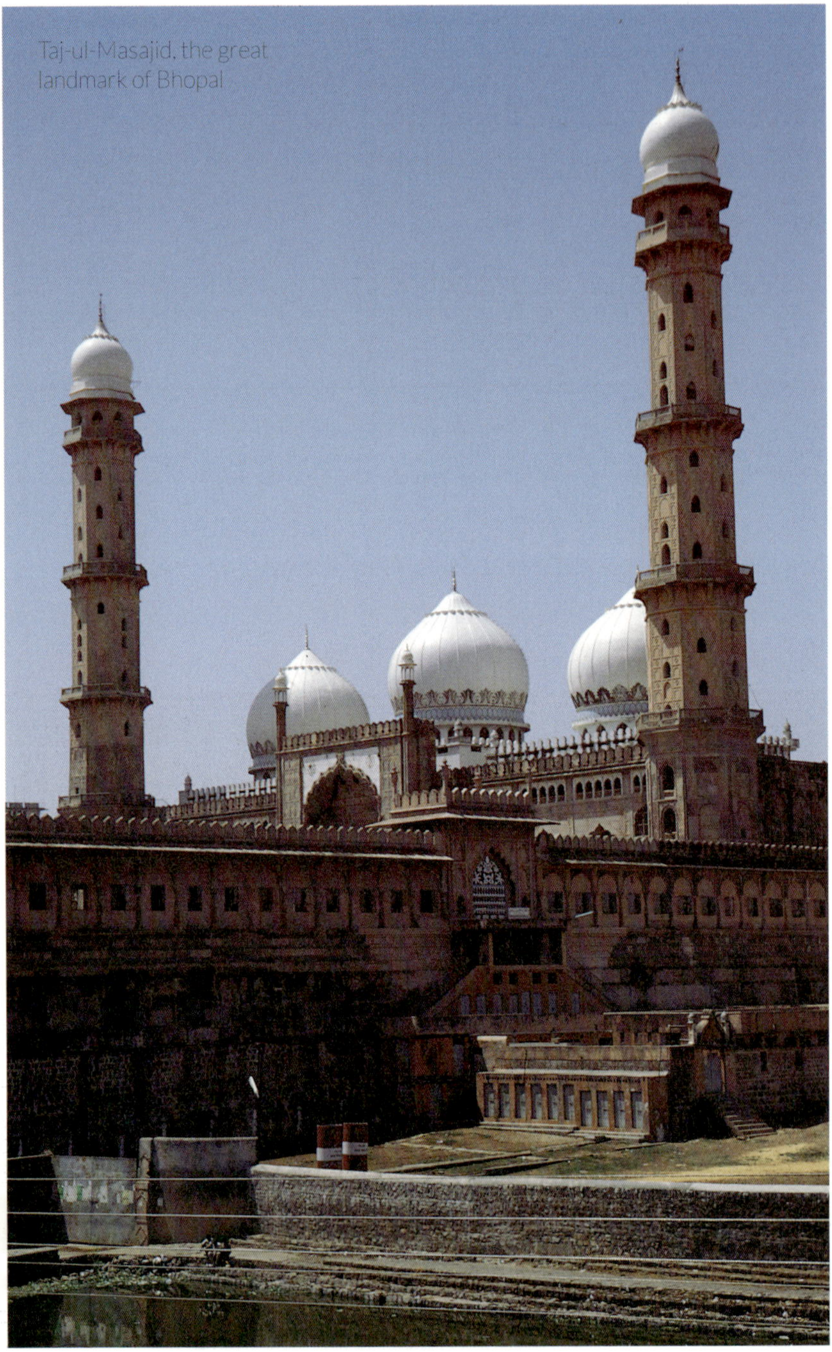

Taj-ul-Masajid, the great landmark of Bhopal

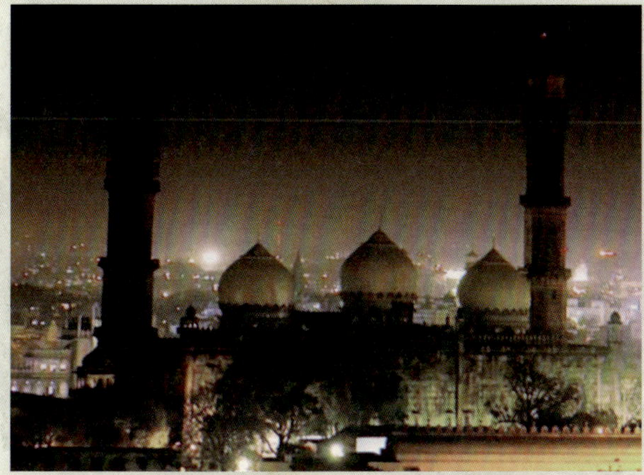

Taj-ul-Masajid at night

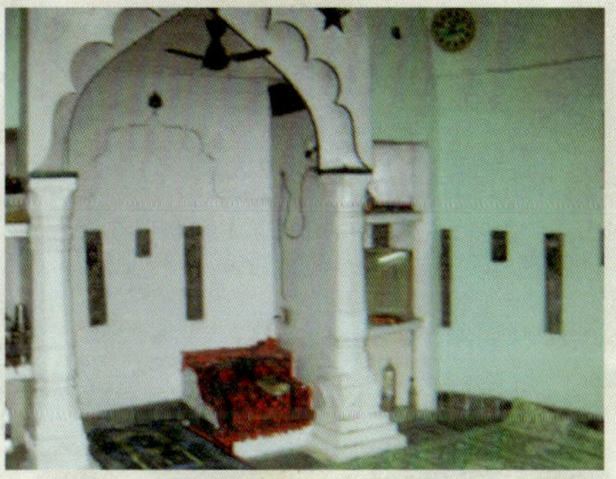

Dhai Seedi ki Masjid

Of the lesser known mosques in Bhopal the Sophia Masjid near the Noor-us Sabah palace, deserves a special mention since within its precinct lie the tombs of Nawab Sultan Jahan Begum and her granddaughter Princess Rabia Sultan, Hon. Major General, Akhtar-e-Hamidia.

Again, perhaps, it may not be out of place to mention that Bhopal also has the smallest mosque in the world with its capacity of just four devotees offering prayers at the same time! It is called the Dhai Seedi ki Masjid which literally means "The mosque of two and a half steps". The tiny mosque stands insignificant and unnoticed on the campus of the Gandhi Medical College and has exactly two and a half flights of stairs to leading inside from its approach road thus justifying its nomenclature. Possibly, it is also the oldest mosque of

Bhopal since it was built about 300 years ago as a makeshift masjid during the construction of Fatehgarh Fort (Bhopal city) by Dost Mohammad Khan so that the guards deployed at the Fort could perform their namaz without disrupting their duty.

Shrines, Legends and Beliefs

Apart from the spectacular mosques the city has several other holy shrines too. Those are the dargahs of the celebrated Pirs of Bhopal, the guardians of the city as the people believe. The most famous of these is the sacred mazar of Pir Mastan Shah, who seems to be the de facto political "high command" of the Bhopal Municipal Corporation. Whosoever gets elected as the chief of the civic board or the mayor, must pay obeisance to the Pir and such has been the tradition. The grave of Pir Mastan Shah lies just outside Sadar Manzil—the headquarters of Bhopal Municipal Corporation, and it is the bounden duty of the city mayor to ensure the proper upkeep of the holy grave. It is also believed that by taking good care of the grave, the sitting mayor earns a fair chance of getting elected a second time. However, the most interesting legend about the supernatural powers of Pir Mastan Shah unfolded during the siege of Bhopal by the Marathas in 1812-1813 that has already been narrated earlier.

The dargah of the Pir Hazrat Shah Ali Shah which is better known as his "Takiya" is located on an island in the centre of the scenic Bada Talab (Upper Lake). The Pir, a Sufi saint of the 18th century lived all alone in the island and his mausoleum was also built there, which is known to never get flooded in spite of rising water level during the monsoon. People regard him as the protector of the city though nobody ever dared to stay there. The legend is that when Maaji

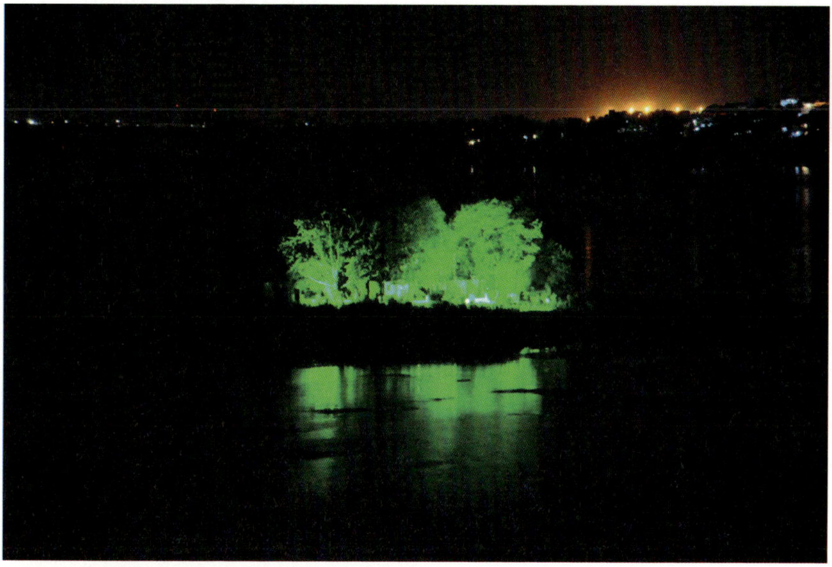

The dargah at Takiya Tapu on Upper Lake in the night

Mamola, the first de facto woman ruler of Bhopal fell seriously ill and slipped into coma, the saint prayed to God to take away his life and spare hers. His wish was granted and Maaji Mamola Bai had recovered while the saint died. Annual Urs in his memory are held at the mazar and people belonging to all faith assemble at the universal congregation in large numbers.

The Khanqah Sharif Mujaddiya at Peer Gate attracts followers from all faiths. During the earlier days even the ruling royals as well as the aristocracy used to throng the holy khanqah to pay homage to the Sufi saint Hazrat Mujaddidi and seek his blessings. The water from the well of this sacred shrine is reputed to have divine healing powers that is said to cure any ailment. Freely available to all, a large number of Hindus and Muslims visit the shrine daily to collect the miraculous water.

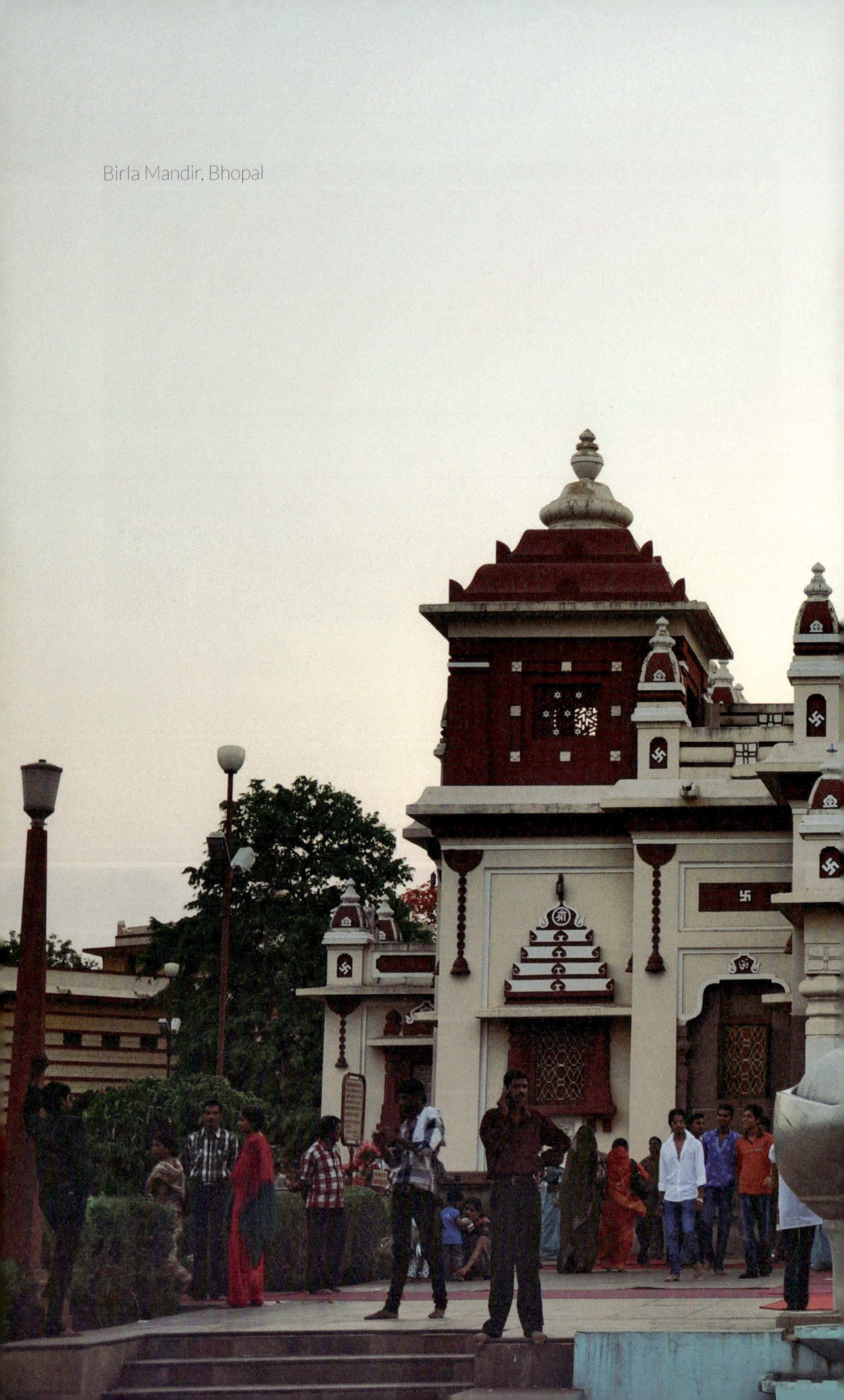

Birla Mandir, Bhopal

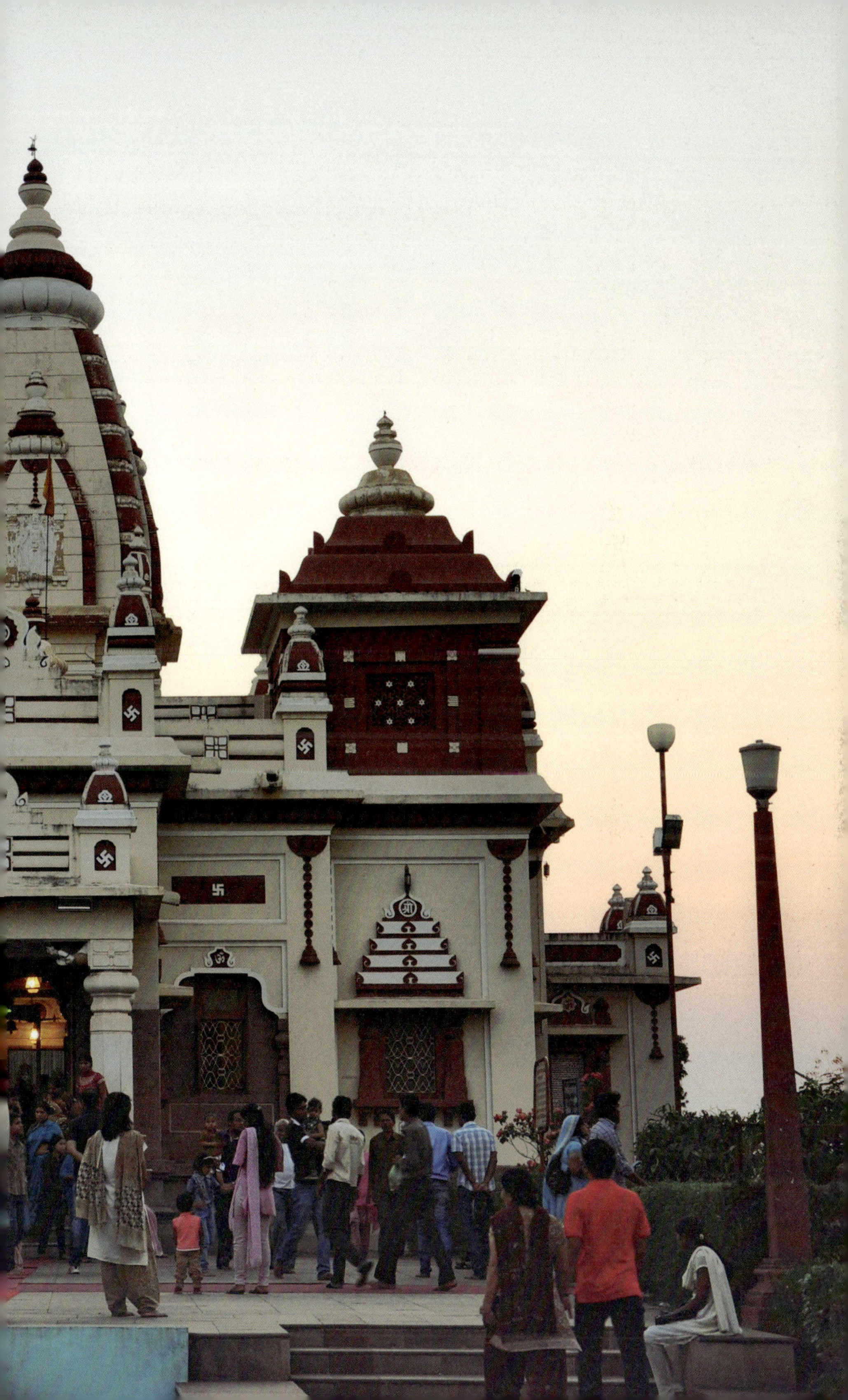

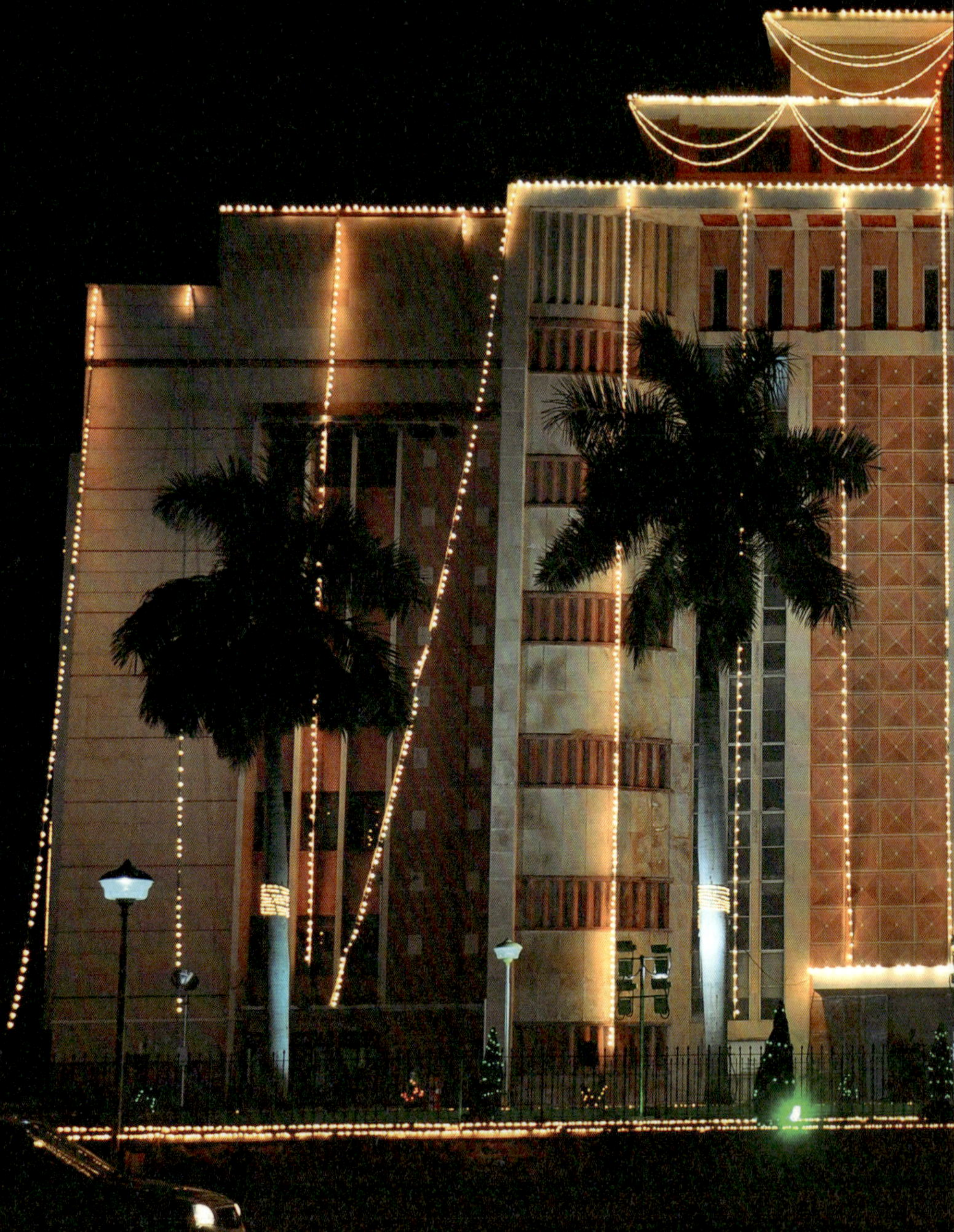

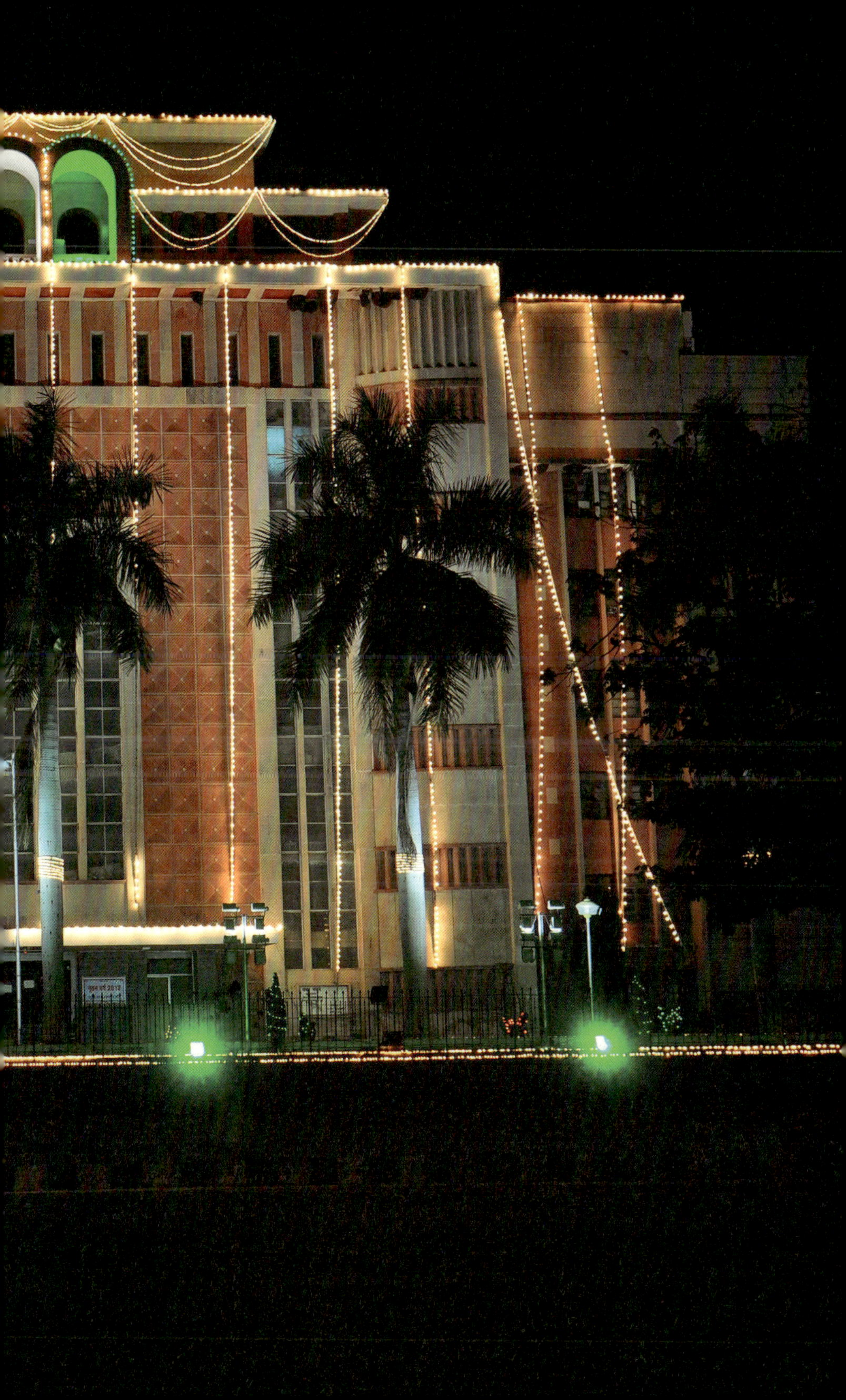

Another shrine near the Peer Gate is known as Pir Sahib-ka-Alam and is situated right outside the residence of a Hindu Agarwal family. The Pir Sahib is considered by all the residents in the locality as their guardian angel. The devoted Agarwals through generations have regarded the Pir as the head of their family and no function is commenced without his blessings.

Raisen, in the outskirts of Bhopal, is an old habitation en route to Sanchi. It is also the sacred resting place of the Sufi saint Pir Hazrat Sharfuddin (Fatehullah Shah), who was the nephew of Khwaja Moinuddin Chisti of Ajmer. Under instructions of the revered Khwaja he came to Raisen along with some followers to quell the prevailing lawlessness in the Malwa region and to promote peace and harmony.

The ruler of Raisen lived in his fort atop a hill well-developed for human habitation, but the upright saint chose to reside below in the jungles at the foothills frequented by wild animals, including the tiger. He never went to visit the fort asking the ruler for favours, instead it was the ruler and other villagers who came to his durbar seeking his blessings. The Pir would always extend his help to all those who were in trouble and went to him expecting some relief; but the Pir could not stand discourtesy. For centuries it had become a convention for all the travellers passing that way to pay courtesy visits to his dargah. As the legend goes, several years ago a state minister nonchalantly went past the dargah without showing the customary respect. As a result, all four tyres of his vehicle burst soon after, and he had to return back all the way to the shrine to atone and apologise to the Pir!

There are also shrines in the old city belonging to other religious faiths, though none is really of major importance. The only exception is the 300-year-old Jain temple on the Idgah hills—a part of Old Bhopal. Connected by a ropeway, this holy shrine also offers a grand panorama of the city, which is an added attraction for the visitors. Major Hindu shrines, mostly built in recent days are located in the newly developed areas of the capital. Notable amongst them are the Hanuman Temple in the Tatya Tope Nagar and the Lakshmi Narayan Temple that was raised on the highest point of the Arera Hills area by one of India's leading Industrialists, the Birlas. From the precincts of the temple one can enjoy the charming panoramic view of the old city. Close to this temple of God is the modern-day temple of democracy—the new Assembly Building or the Vidhan Sabha called Vallabh Bhawan. It was designed by the celebrated architect Charles Correa. Another shrine of historical importance is the first Catholic Church in Bhopal known as the cathedral of St. Francis of Assisi. It was constructed by the French Bourbons who occupied high, influential positions in the courts of the first two nawab begums. In those days it happened to be a rare example of religious tolerance and amity for an Islamic state to allow a church to come up and flourish with provisions of a cemetery as well as a missionary school.

By-lanes and Bazars

At first glance, the present-day city of Old Bhopal may appear like any other haphazardly grown, small and congested town, hardly having any distinct character to attract travellers. However, to discover and enjoy any unknown place, such as Old Bhopal in particular, the best way would be to explore it slowly and gradually while roaming on foot along the city's uncharted, serpentine, narrow streets, dingy lanes and by-lanes. In reality, most of the crowded pathways in the old city are inaccessible for any vehicles other than the ubiquitous two wheelers that can move with strange dexterity amidst the chaos all around. Having an inherent small-town feel the old city possesses a certain quaint picturesque charm about it. The city and bazar has neither a delineated beginning nor a well-defined end. A stranger has to find his way crawling amidst the endless jostling crowd, and at the same time taking care of himself; at places he may also have to manoeuvre heaps of the saleable sundry articles lying scattered on his way. If willing to explore further he should be leaving behind the huge old mosques, by-passing the many lesser shrines, some eateries, small industries and varied odd shops on either side. Street vendors will beckon at their wares while the shop-boys would keep yelling to sell every kind of goods.

Within a labyrinth of such roads, the old city of Bhopal encompasses its famous mosques, palaces and other heritage sites.

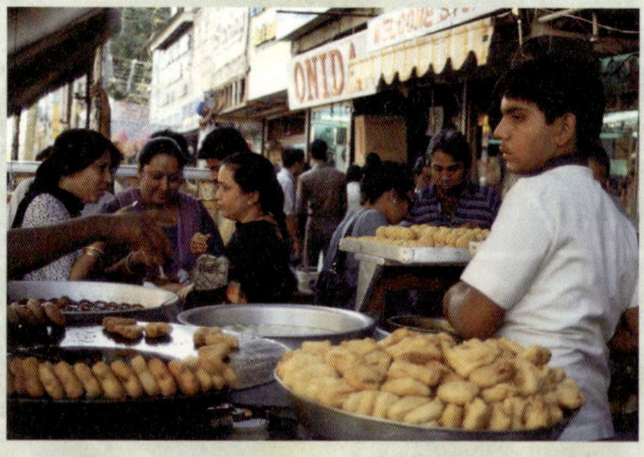

An eatery at Chowk Bazar, Old Bhopal

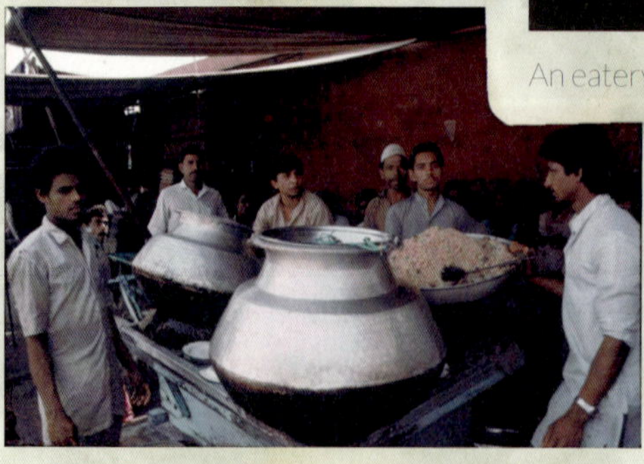

A roadside eatery in Old Bhopal

And indeed it is here, that one can truly grasp, feel and discover the essence of the city.

No doubt, the central market place of Chowk Bazar is a miniature crowded maze. Again, it is also the place where one can find and buy every possible consumer goods one can imagine. Bellowing with life each side of the road is chock-a-block, full of shops. Besides the state government emporium Mrignayani, Chowk Bazar is the real shopping destination where one can get the choicest specialities of textiles such as Tussor silk, Chanderi and Maheshwari sarees. Beaded glass artistry artifacts on velvet, silver and golden zardozi embroidered articles are available aplenty in the Chowk Bazar and such items can be bargained for a reasonable value. But one has to be careful so as to be able to sort the wheat from the chaff.

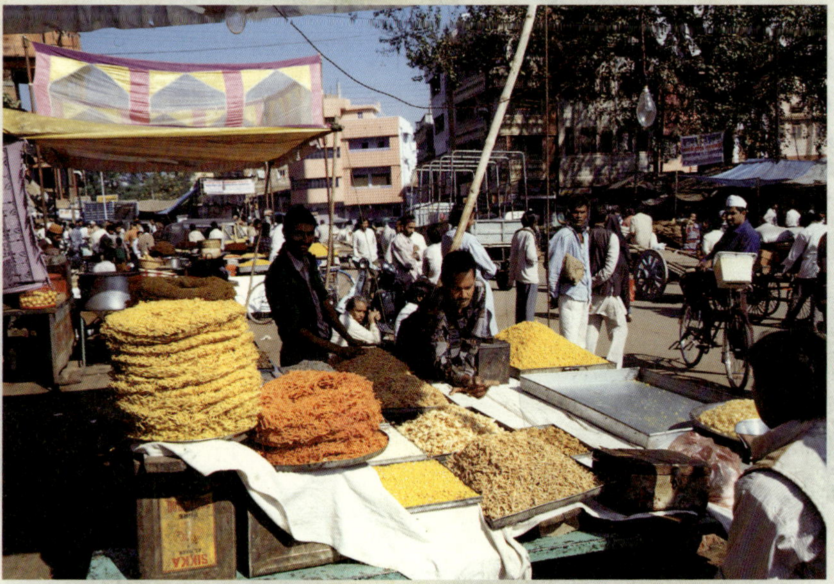

Eid declicacies displayed at a roadside stall

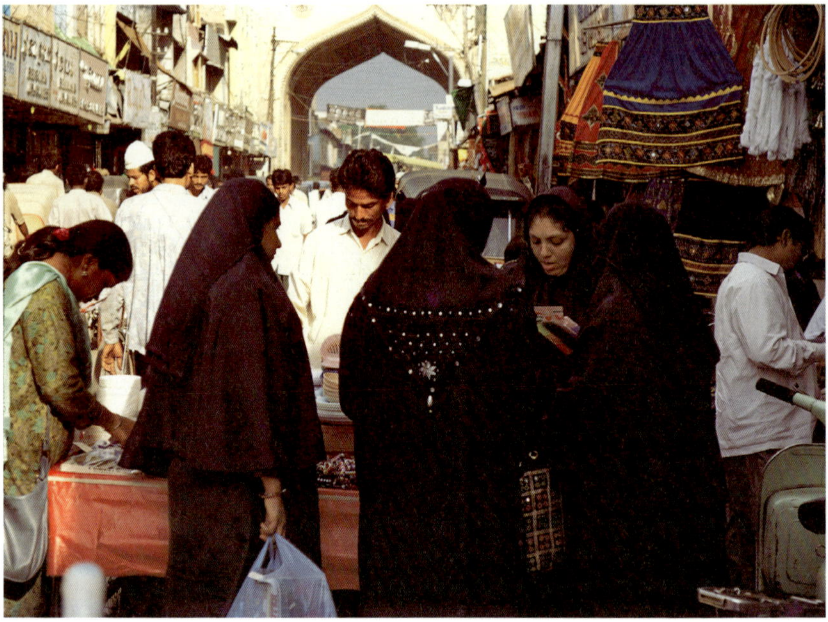

Chowk Bazar

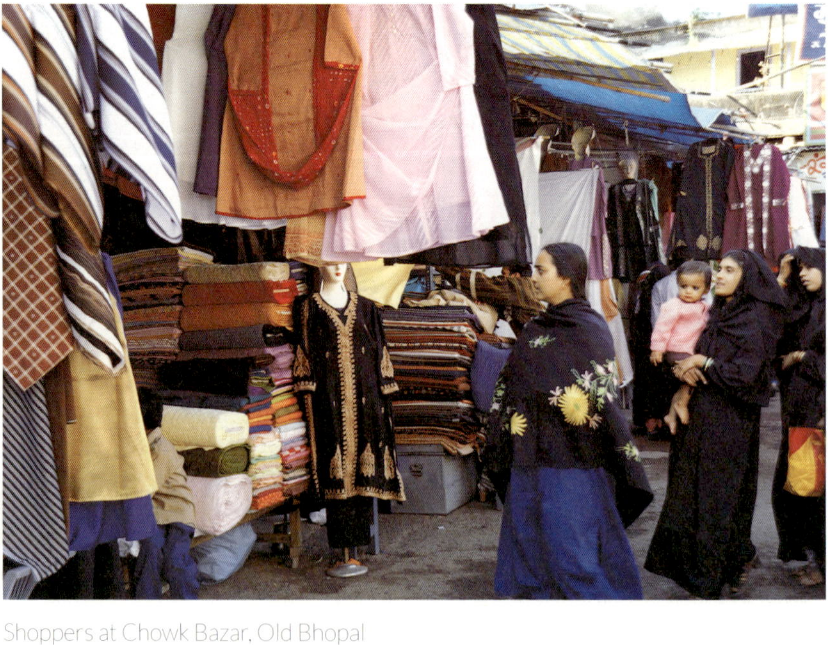

Shoppers at Chowk Bazar, Old Bhopal

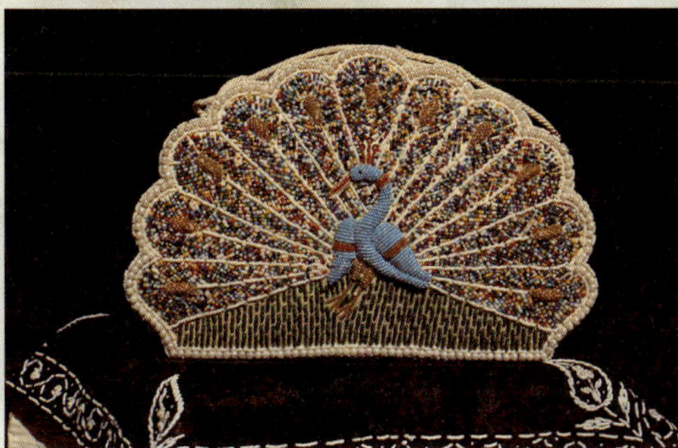

Glass-bead embroidery work on a tea cosy

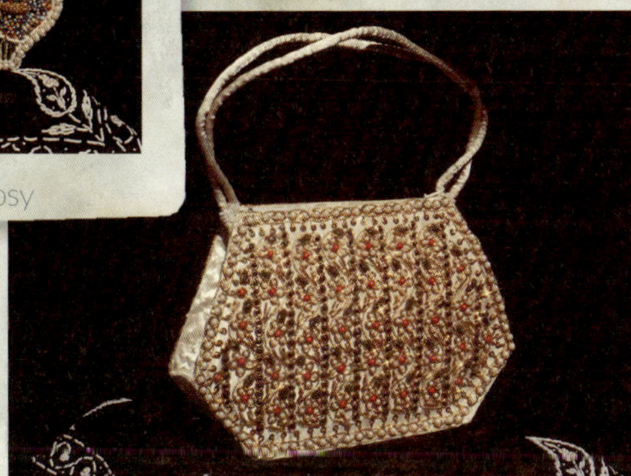

An exquisite ladies purse in zari work

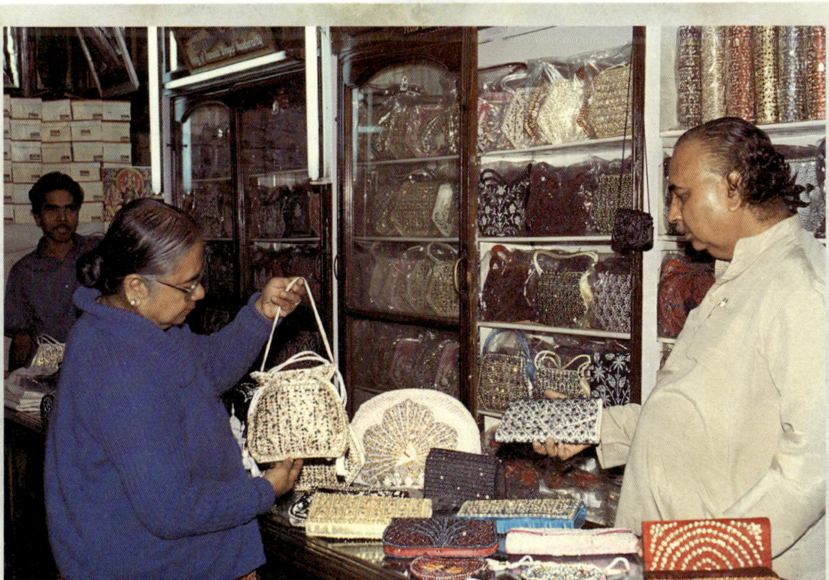

Zari-embroidered articles at a shop, Chowk Bazar

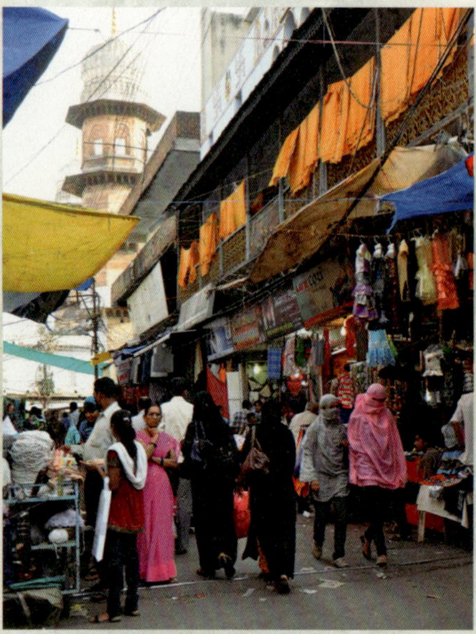

Chowk Bazar

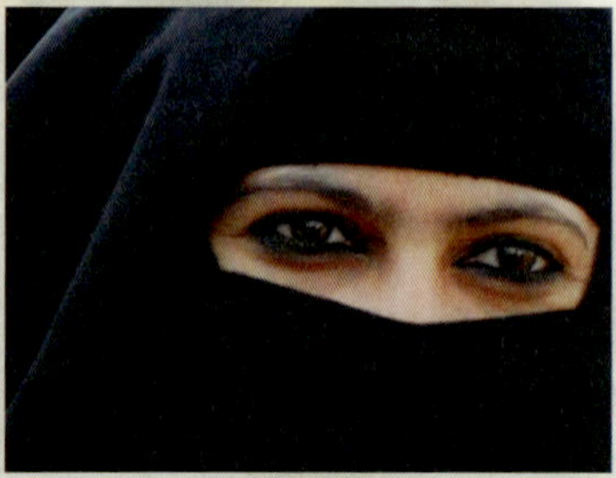

A veiled face in Chowk Bazar

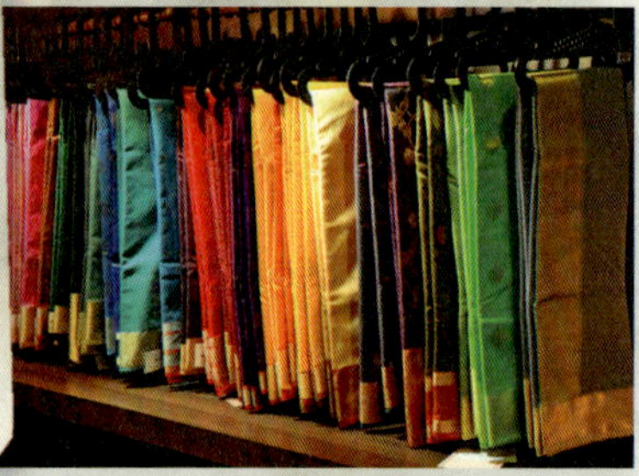

Mrignayanee showroom, GTB Complex

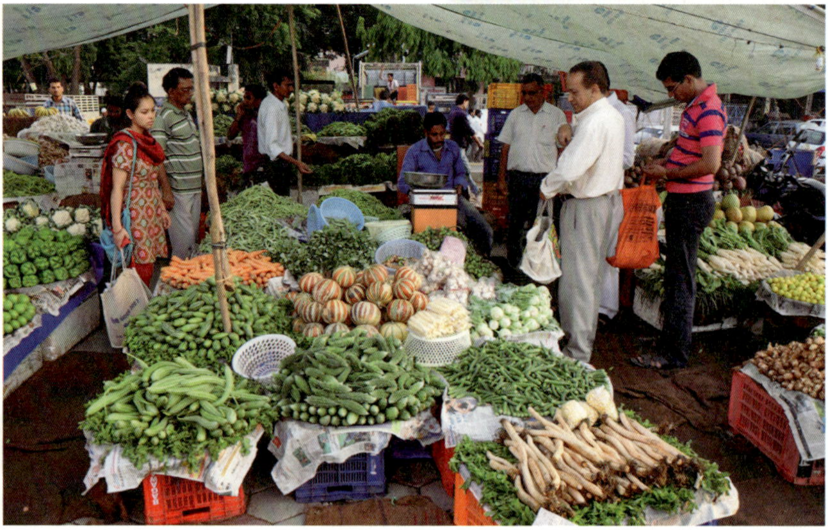

Bittan Market Haat

Industry and Township

The northern part of the old city contains the sprawling large industrial suburb, and the humongous residential slum that has grown around as its part through the years. It was here on the fateful night of 2 December 1984, that an unprecedented catastrophe befell, defaming the name of Bhopal throughout the world. It was the worst ever industrial disaster of the world in which a storage tank of the nearby plant of the Union Carbide Corporation containing a highly poisonous chemical known as methyl isocyanate, had burst emitting a deadly cloud of the fatal gas that instantly killed numerous unwary, poor inhabitants of the nearby slum in their sleep. By the time the gaseous poisoning cloud had dispersed, over 2,000 people were already dead and over a lakh others affected became partially disabled for life. Many more thousands died in the aftermath and those who survived too suffered from severe health repercussions. In all, the great

A view of the upcoming township of Bhopal

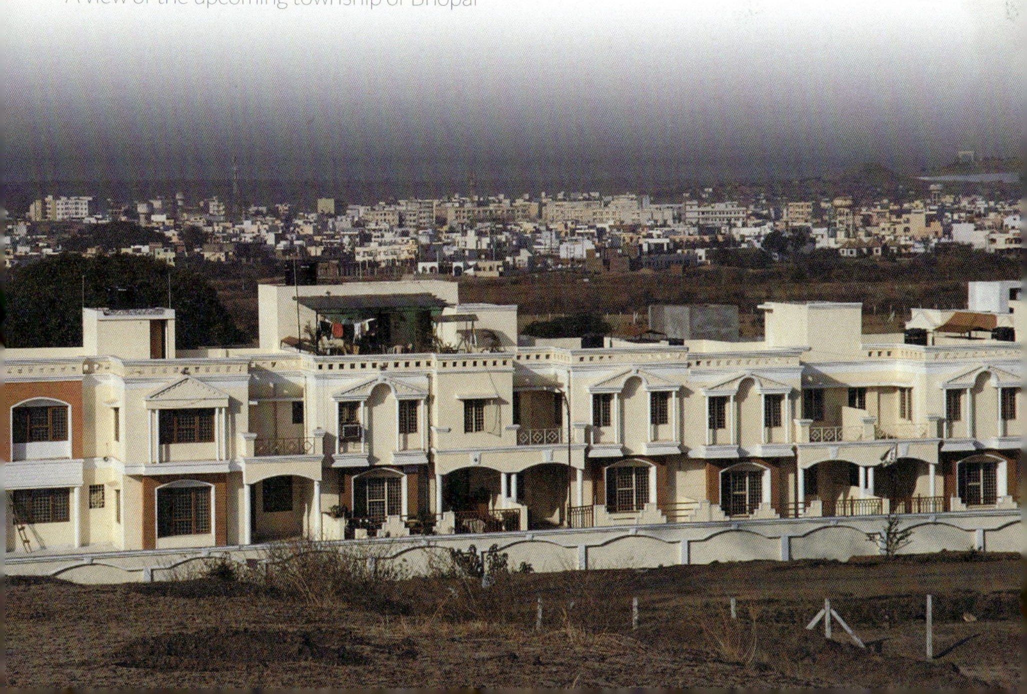

disaster had affected about 3,00,000 people or more. As for compensation, the foreign company owning the plant had just paid a meagre amount after much haggling and inordinate delay and went scot-free, thanks to their tricky manipulations! A legal battle is still continuing against the company officials in the International Court of Law.

Again, on the outskirts of New Bhopal, bordering the south-east, lies the sprawling establishment and township of Bharat Heavy Electricals Limited (BHEL); it is an electrical heavy power plant machinery manufacturing concern, the largest in the country and the only big industry of Bhopal. Founded as an autonomous body in 1962, BHEL is an undertaking of the Government of India and operates as the only major engineering company fabricating integrated heavy power plant equipments having a worldwide market. Apart from the large township of BHEL, many other satellite towns are growing up around the fast expanding capital and they all abound with varied small scale industries.

Though the Begums' antique citadel is overpopulated, the new city that came up primarily after Bhopal's glorious crowning as the state capital in 1956, is a modern township. The sprawling new Bhopal in the western part of the capital has wide avenues, sleek high-rise office buildings, beautifully gardened residential bungalows, dazzling shiny markets and glamorous modern malls. Major parts of this posh and ever expanding area interspersed with charming parks and profuse greenery is known as Arera Colony that also boasts of its own waterfront, the beautiful though small Shahpura Lake. Besides, there are well-developed new localities like Tatya Tope Nagar, Shivaji Nagar and Malviya Nagar, etc.

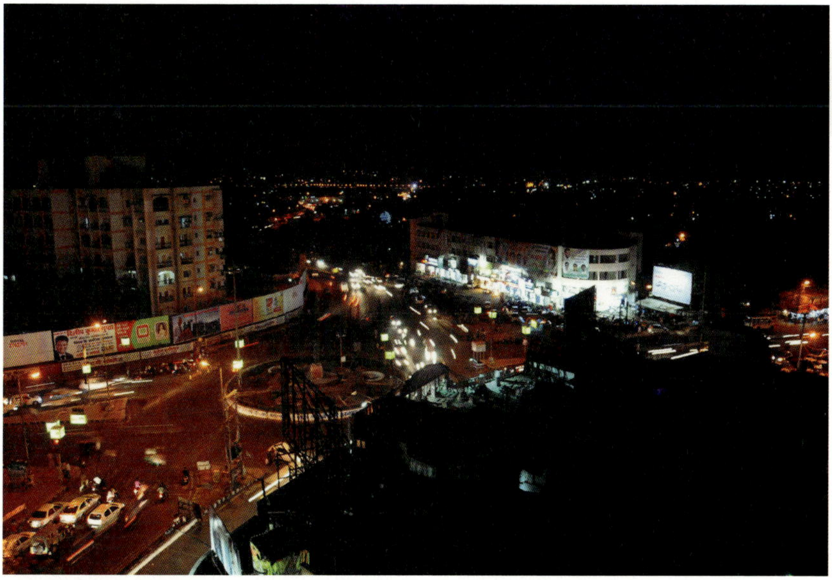

New Market, TT Nagar at night

Sindhi people displaced from Pakistan have their own colony, Sant Hidaram Nagar in Bairagarh to the west of Bhopal.

Nature's Bounty

The new city has several scenic gardens and well-maintained parks with lovely green meadows, old shady trees and leafy bowers. Among them the best is Mayur Park, developed along either side of the Link Road that connects Maharana Pratap Nagar and New Market. The superb garden is beautifully planned with water pool, lovely flower beds, green bushes and shady trees. The charm is further enhanced by the undulating grassy terrain. Of the other interesting parks, most notable is the Chinar Garden where small trees and bushes attract attention for being imaginatively pruned in various shapes; these are again nicely interspersed with

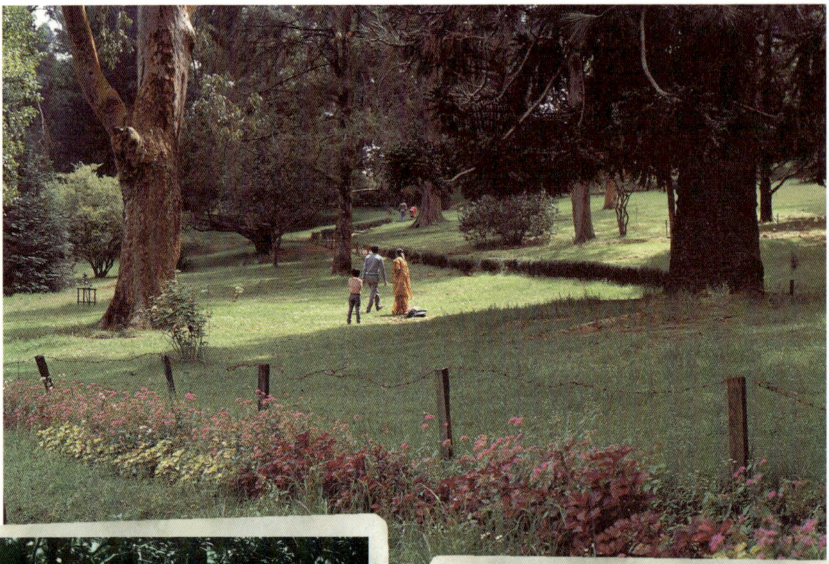

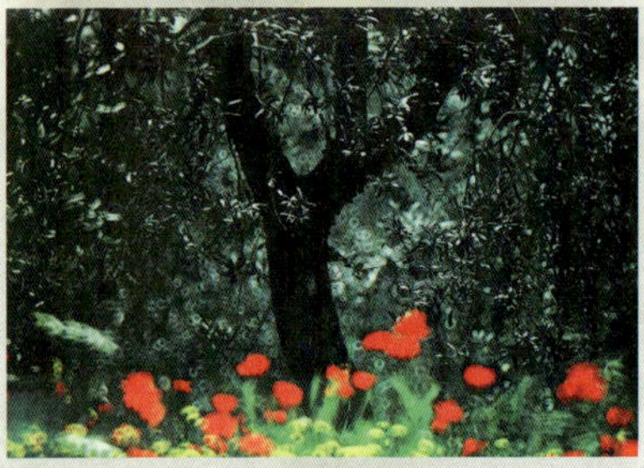

Mayur Park (this and above)

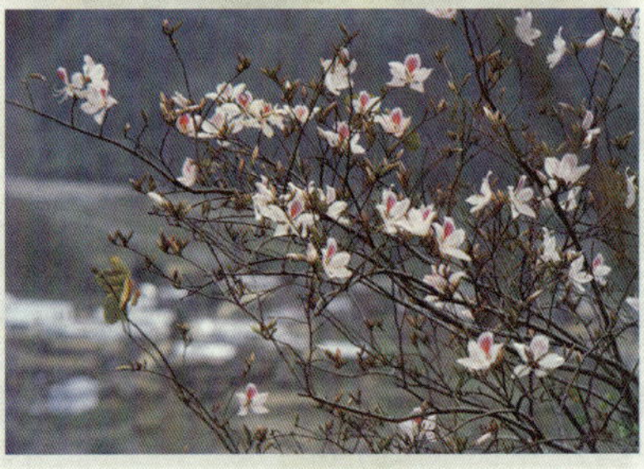

A tree in full blossom in Mayur Park

strange and wonderful pieces of art installations made from redundant scrap materials. But gardens are just trivial human creations, planned and reared artificially as retreats or diversions from the daily boredom of city life.

Beyond the periphery of city's concrete clusters, Nature reveals her ever-bountiful beauty in the many dales and glades lying all around rustic Bhopal. Here, at the end of wintry days, one would never miss to note the advent of spring as heralded by a sudden all-pervading fiery flush brought about overnight by the golden red Flame of the Forest or the splendours of blossoming Palash. Then comes summer—the months for the never-fading crimson Gulmohurs on trees without leaves! Thereafter arrives the season of monsoon and its harbinger, the abundance of golden yellow Amaltas in grape-like clusters. In the precincts of posh leafy bungalows a common sight is the profusion of charming splashes of blue Jacarandas. On the ground level too there would be numerous beautiful wild flowers in varied shades of colour and shape within the bushes and amongst the road-side shrubs. Over and above all these are the ubiquitous Bougainvilleas in multiple hues of red, orange, magenta and white.

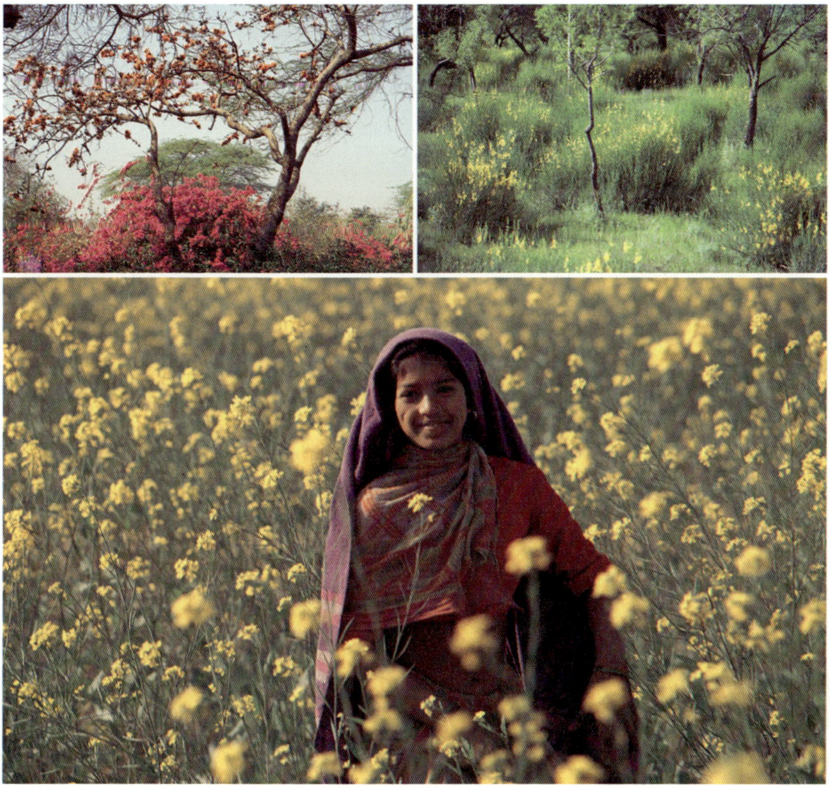

Spring in rural Bhopal (all above)

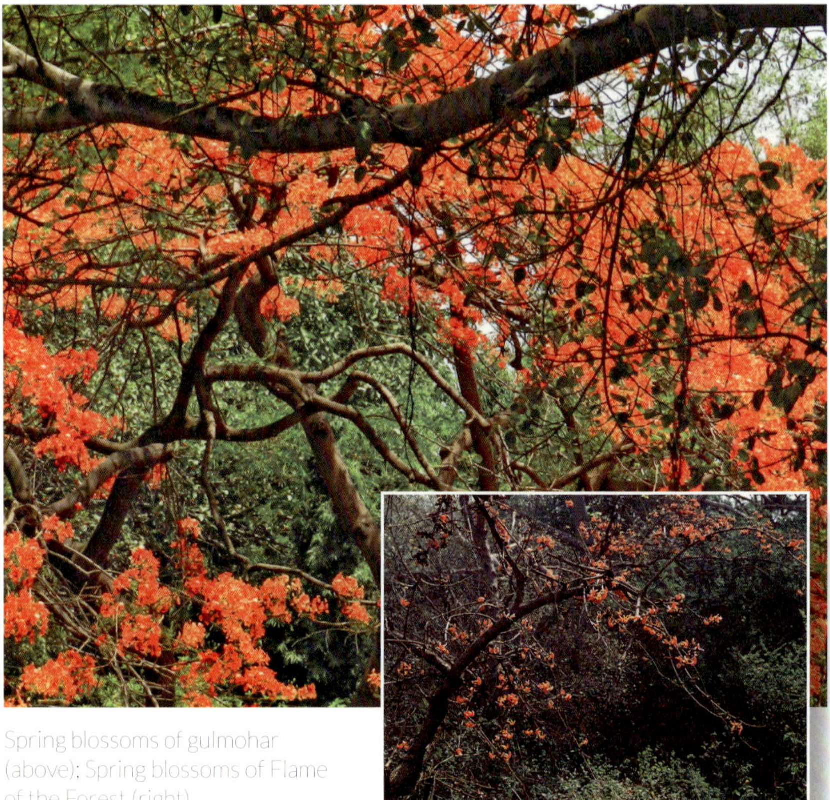

Spring blossoms of gulmohar (above); Spring blossoms of Flame of the Forest (right)

It is but natural that given the adequate forest cover which Bhopal possesses till now, one should find many species of birds. Bereft of large trees, Begums' Bhopal has just plenty of pigeons, largely inhabiting the Jama Masjid area as they prefer living in the vicinity of human habitats. However, the green new Bhopal has plenty of the avian fauna; the most common of these are the fidgety brown robins and the red-vented bulbuls who feel least afraid of humans. The only missing bird is the common crow which surprisingly is a rare sight in Bhopal. Colourful kingfishers, egrets large and small, and the lanky lapwings are often seen around the roadside pools and wherever there is some accumulation of rainwater.

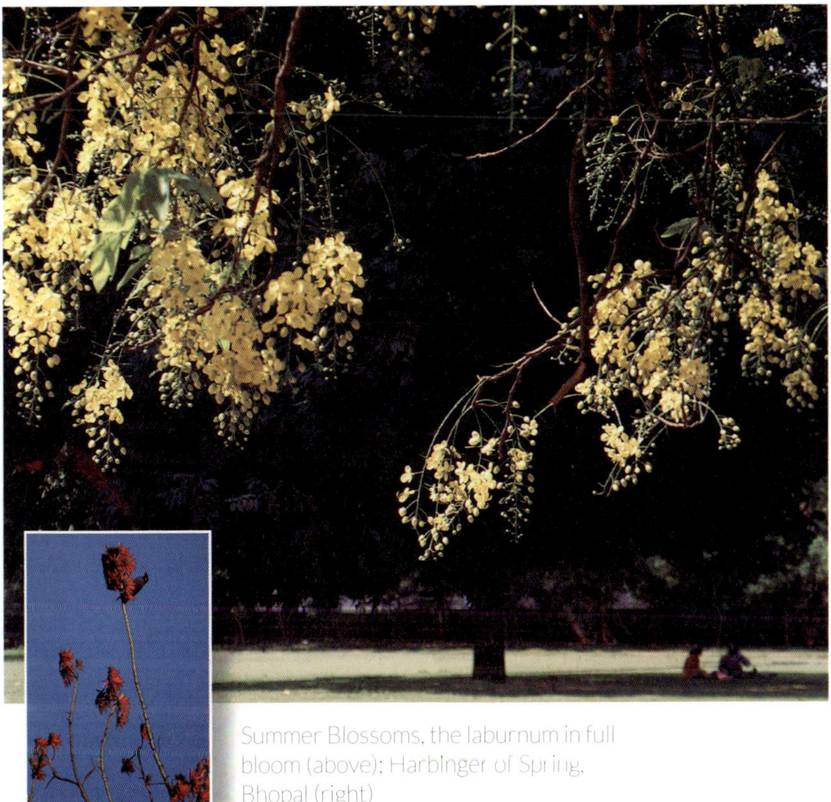

Summer Blossoms, the laburnum in full bloom (above); Harbinger of Spring, Bhopal (right)

At the base area of Shamla hills bordering the Upper Lake is yet another interesting site—the Van Vihar National Park. Covering an area of 4.5 sq. km it was founded in 1983 and is now being further developed as a modern zoological park where animals enjoy free movement in their natural habitat. The carnivores like tiger, lion, panther, bear, hyena, python and crocodiles are kept within a vast open territory with fencing at the boundary; the herbivores like cheetal, black buck, blue bull, swamp deer and others roam about freely on the open grassland. Also, about 200 species of avian fauna—many of them being migratory, inhabit the Van Vihar and its marshy wetland areas. Other than the small Guindy National Park of

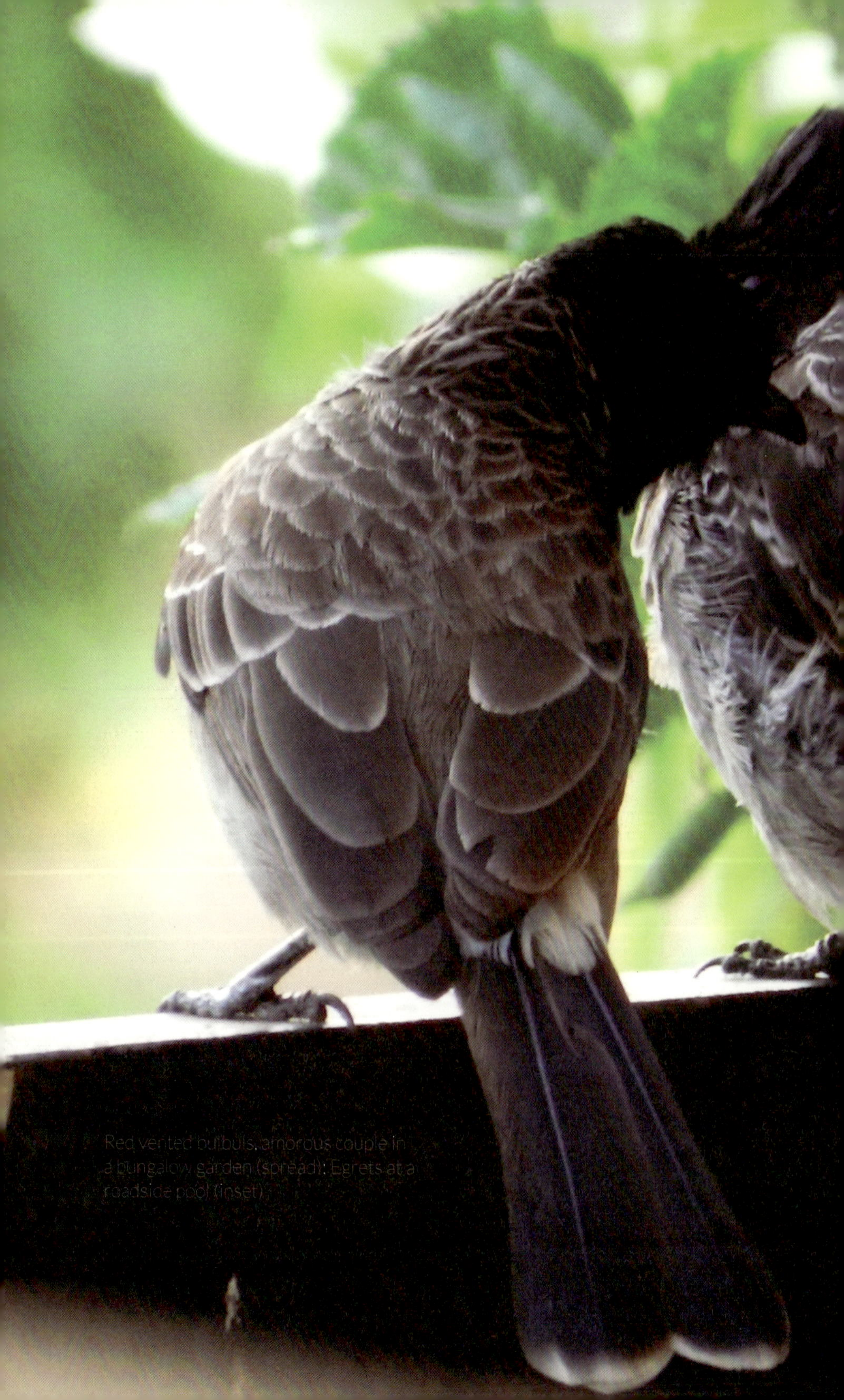

Red vented bulbuls, amorous couple in a bungalow garden (spread); Egrets at a roadside pool (inset)

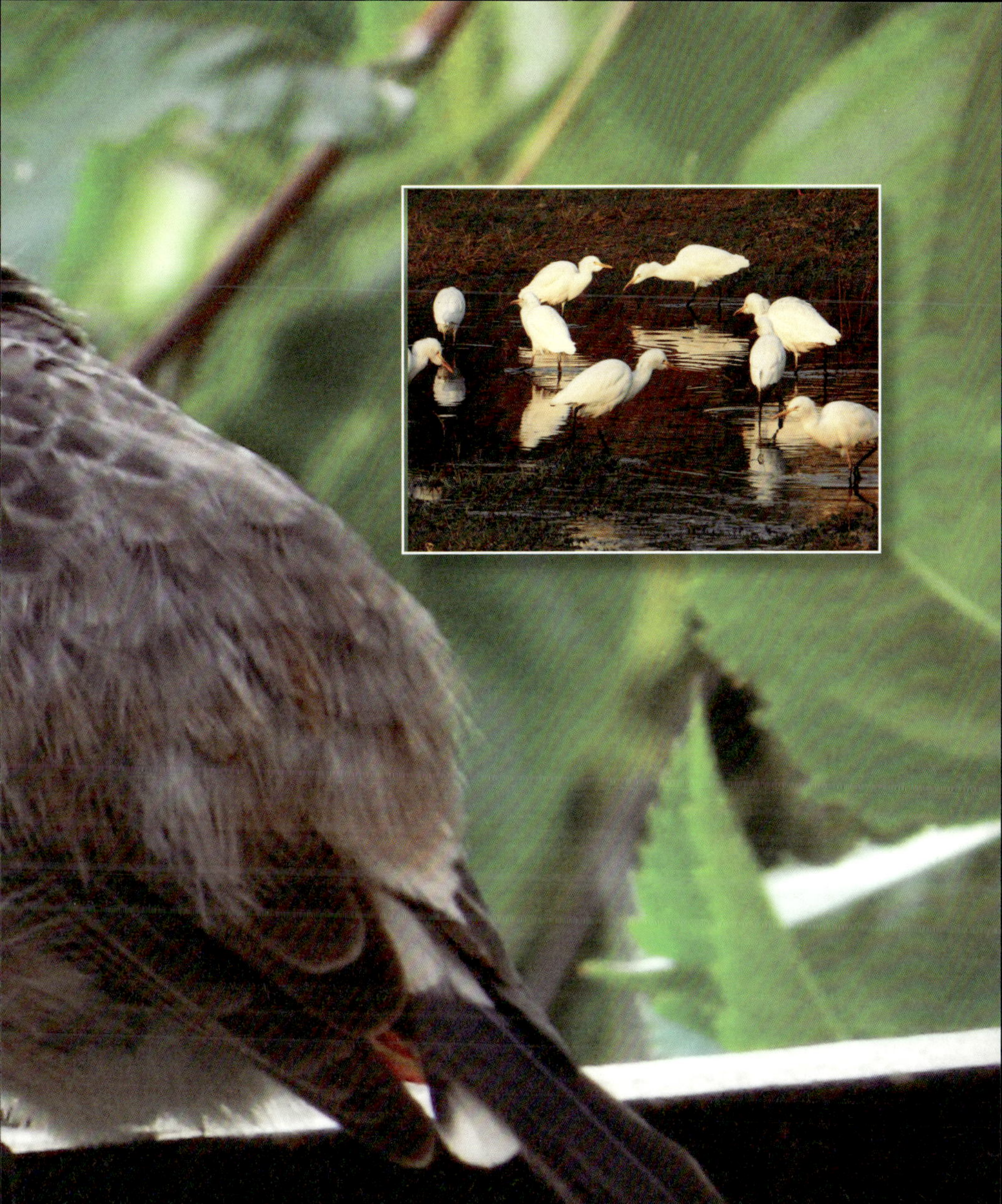

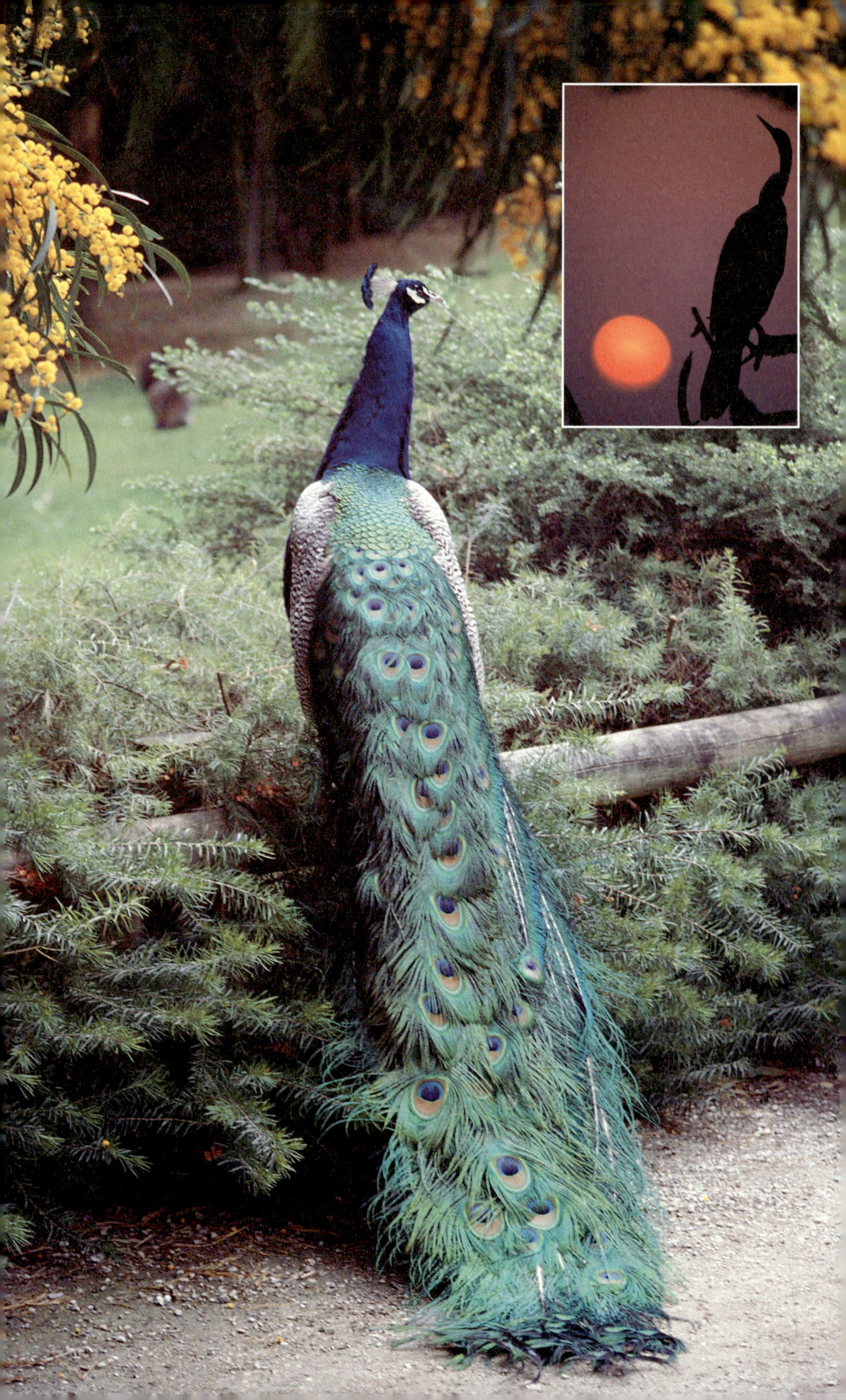

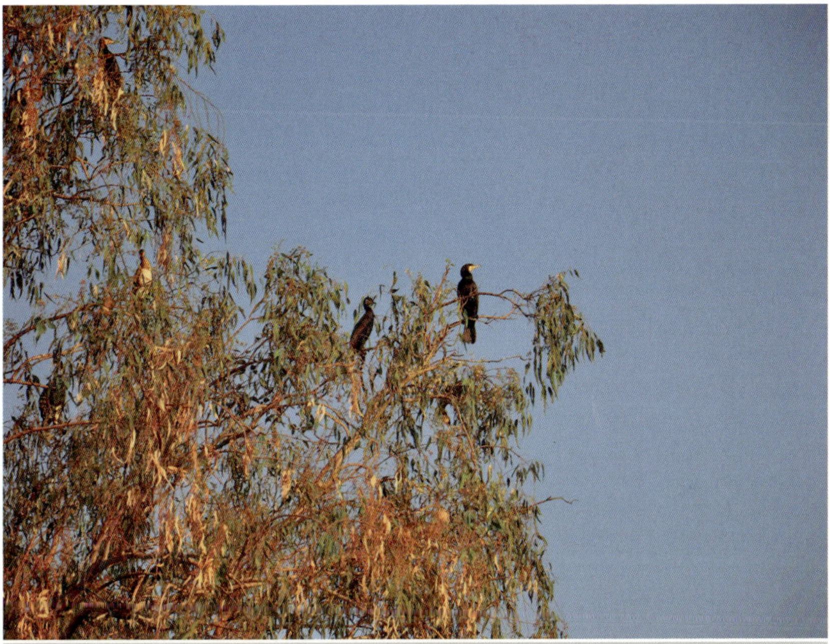

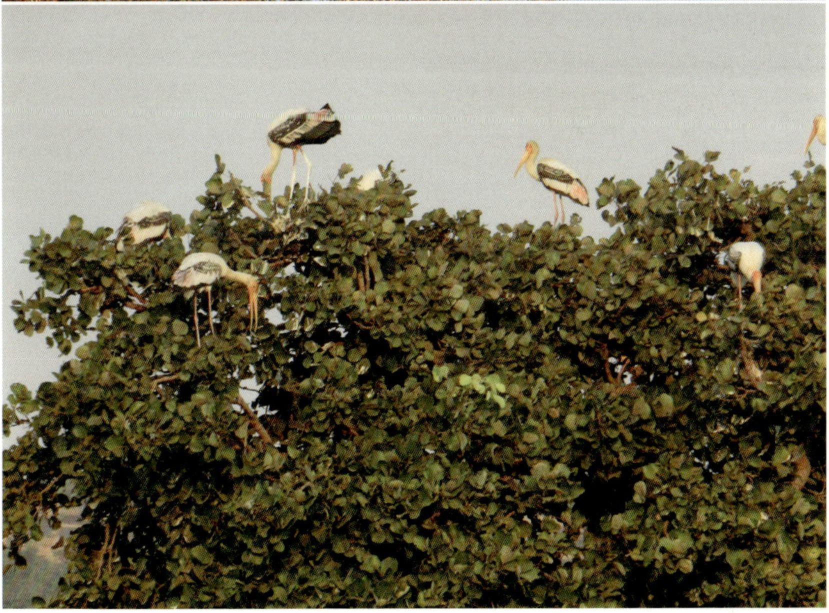

Cormorants at Van Vihar National Park (above); Painted Storks, Van Vihar National Park (below); A snake bird at Van Vihar National Park (inset); A peacock at Van Vihar National Park (facing page)

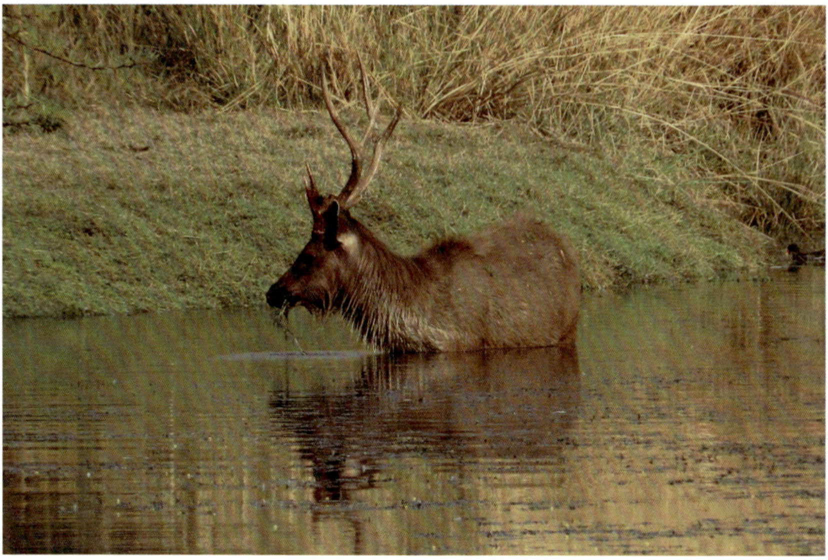

Swamp deer in Van Vihar National Park

Chennai, no other city in India can boast of having a similar wildlife habitat at its very centre.

City of Lakes

Known as the "city of lakes", Bhopal has several of them in and around the city. The charming Bada Talab or the Upper Lake dominating the capital is over one thousand year old and perhaps is the oldest manmade lake in India. Created by the Paramara king Raja Bhoj in early 11th century the lake has earthen dams at several locations. This 14 sq. km spread Upper Lake is an offshoot of the much bigger lake created at Bhojpur that was called Bhim Kund or Sagar Tal and occupied 650 sq. km area. Built over the river Betwa and supported by a massive dam it was certainly the largest manmade lake in the country, if not in the world. Unfortunately, the dam was demolished in the 15th century by Sultan Hoshang Shah.

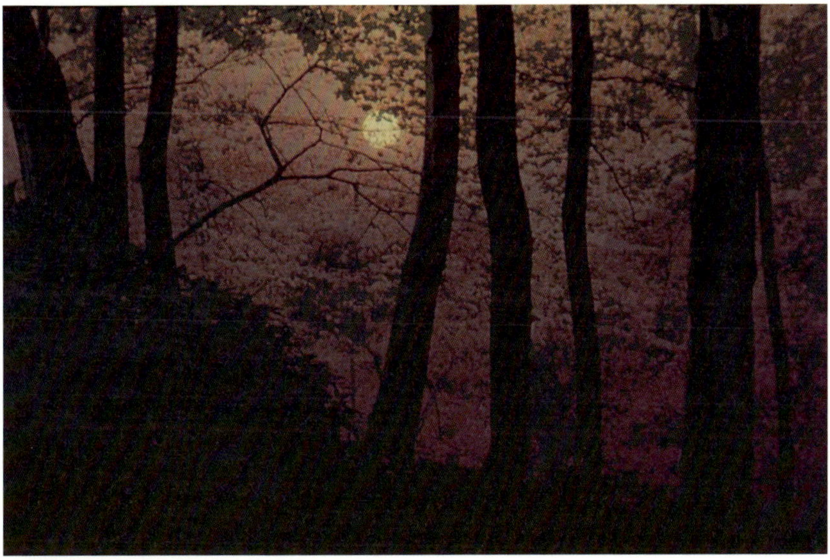

Sunrise, Upper Lake

When Nawab Hayat Mohammad Khan (1777-1807) felt the need to expand the city, he made a dam on the Ban Ganga river building the first ever bridge of Bhopal—the Pul Pukhta. The stone bridge, 300 yards long and 23 yards wide, also acted as a check-dam and created the Chhota Talab or the Lower Lake. No major settlements were established in the area till Nawab Jahangir Mohammad Khan (1837-1844), set up the cantonment of Jahangirabad. Later in 1874, when Nawab Shah Jahan Begum created her city called Shahjahanabad, three more small terraced lakes, all inter-connected, had to be created—Motia Talab, Noor Mahal Talab and Hussaini Talab. These lakes were dependent on seasonal rains and an additional reservoir had to be constructed to maintain the balance as well as the level of water in these lakes. It was an elaborate system of brick-lined vaulted drains that collected and channelised water into the lakes. The channels had been transformed into splashing fountains and gurgling cascades,

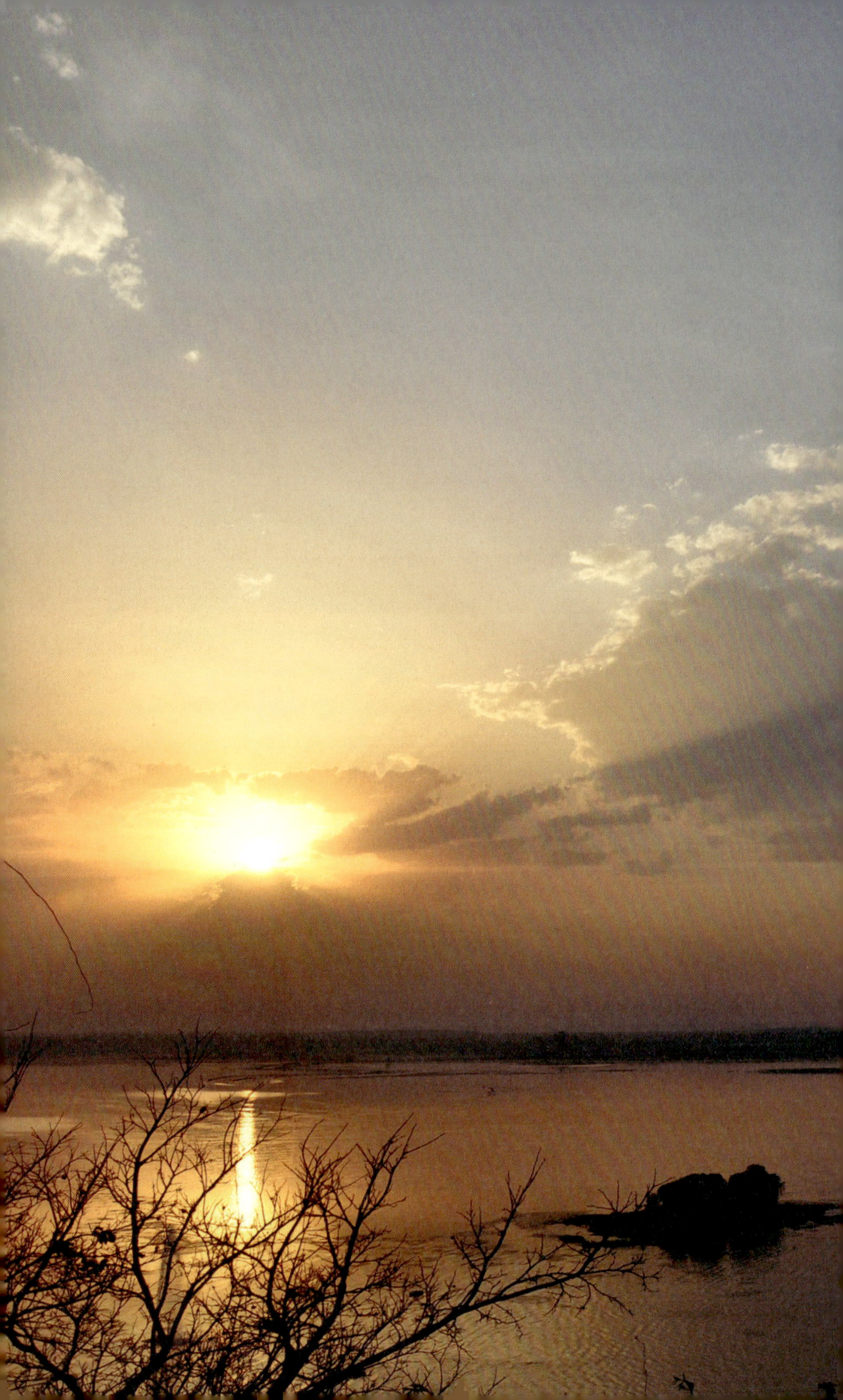

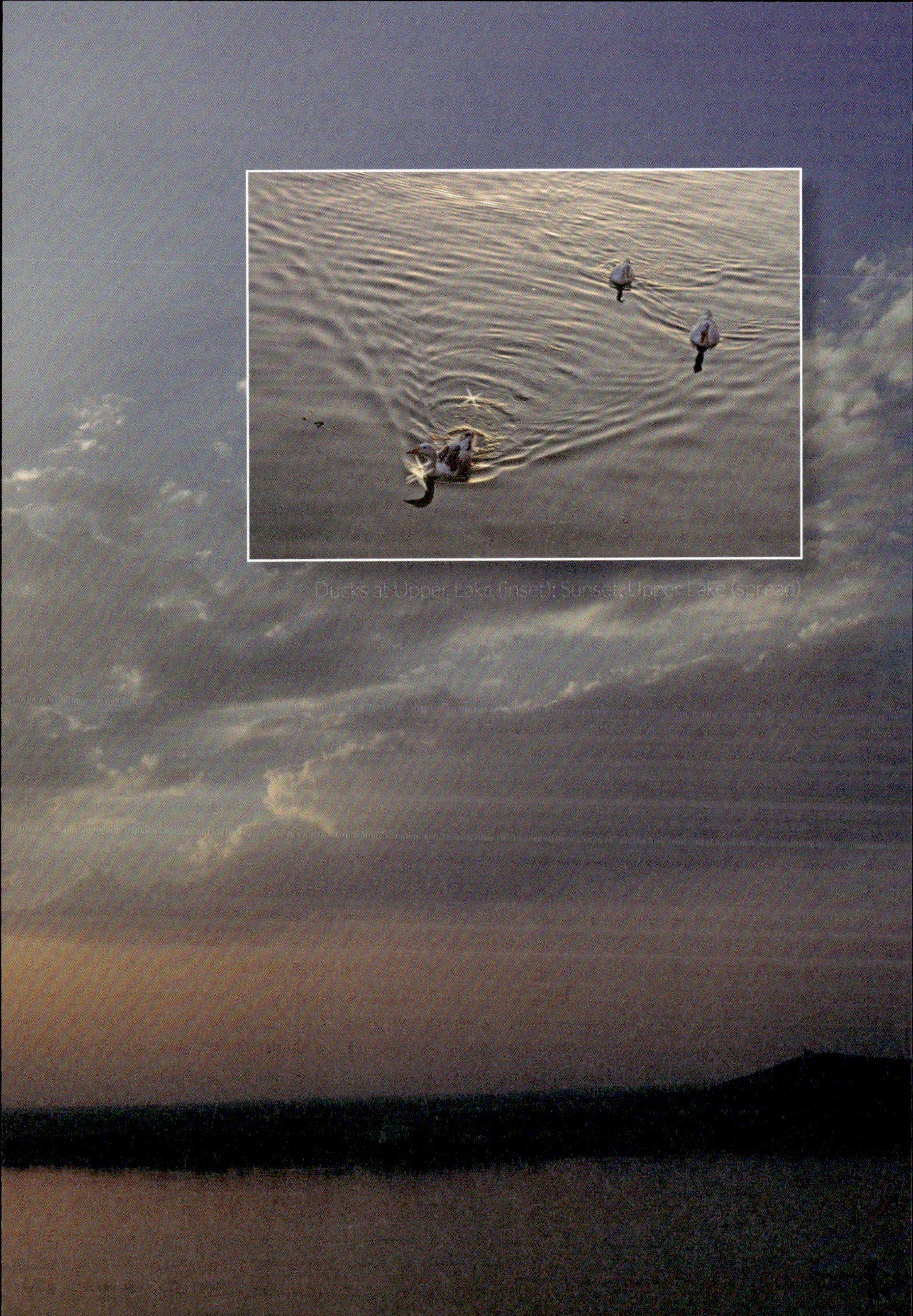

Ducks at Upper Lake (inset); Sunset, Upper Lake (spread)

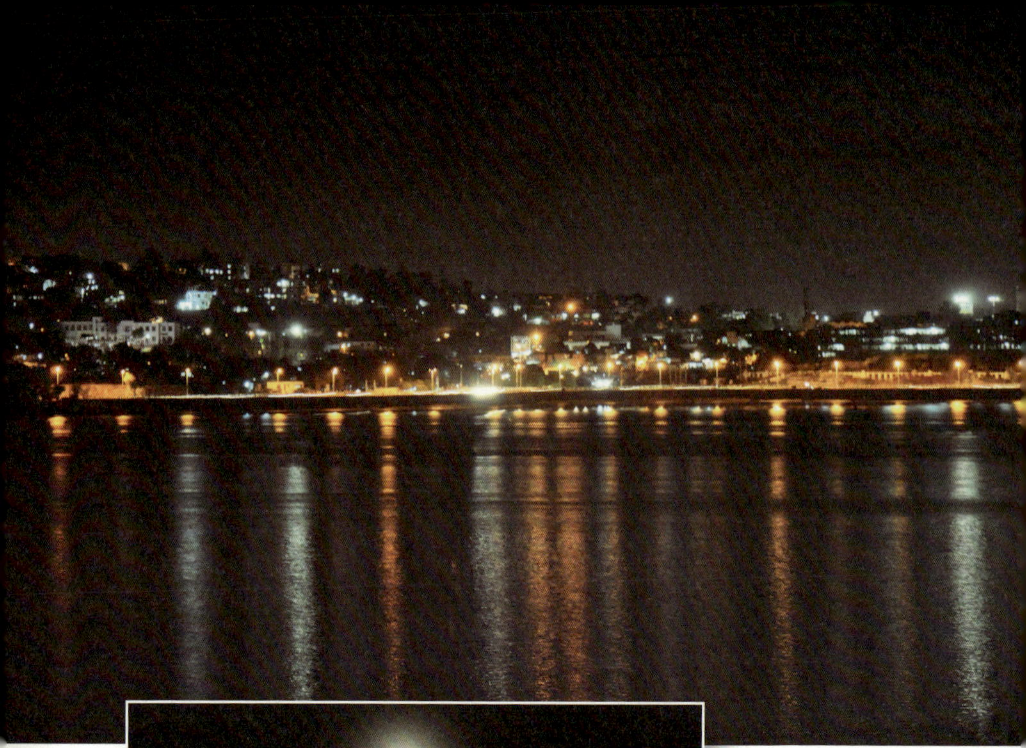

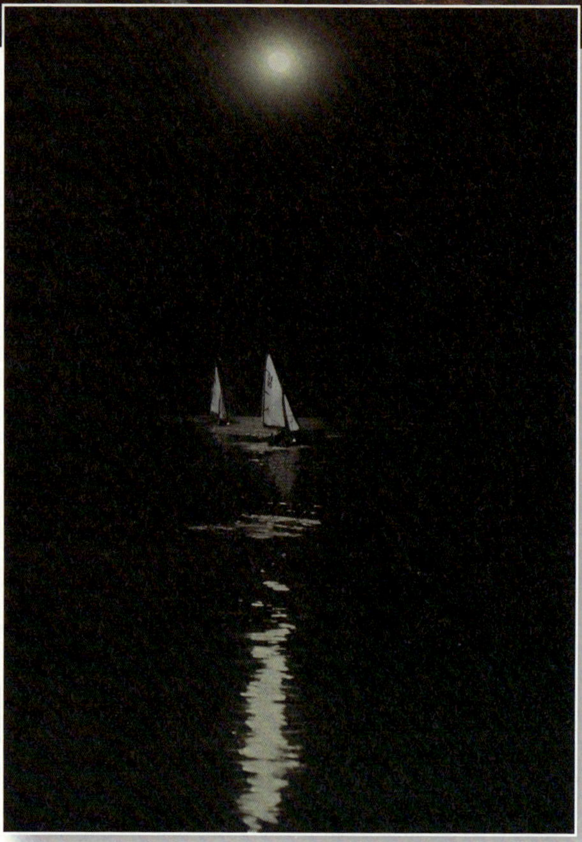

VIP Road over the lake at night (above); Moonlit view of Upper Lake (left)

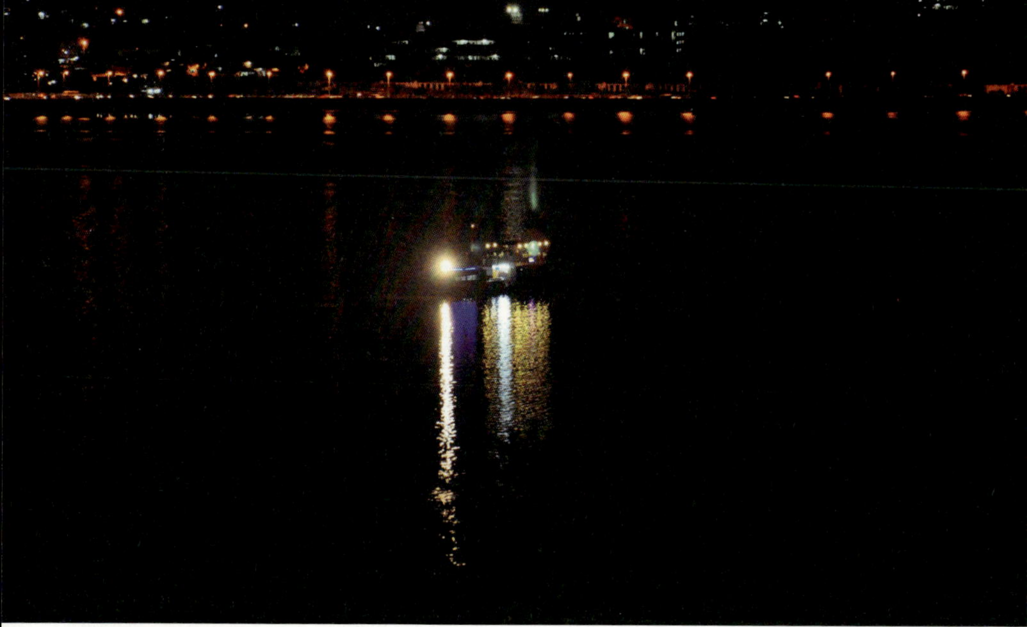

Upper Lake at night

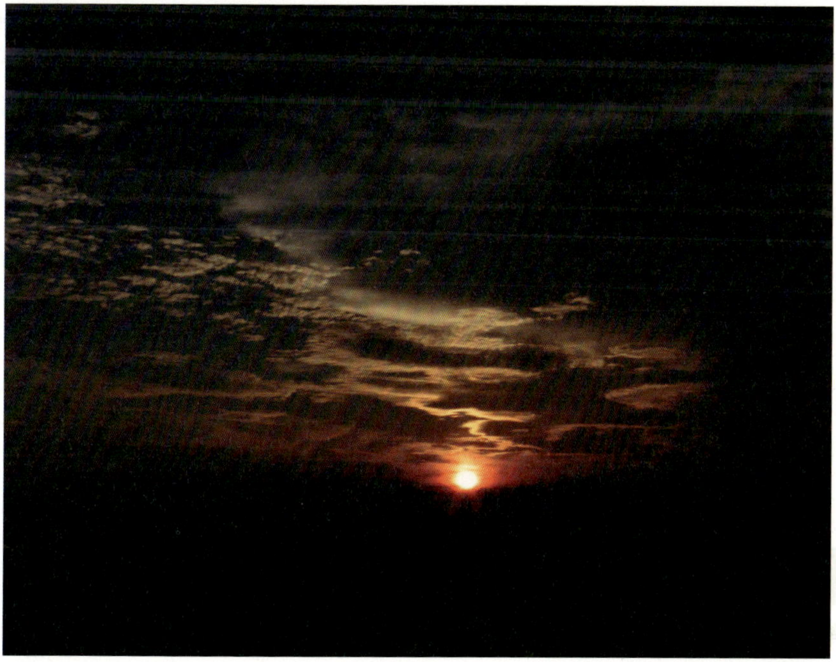

A Glorious sunset over the Upper lake

all perfumed with rose water and fragrant essence of kewda (exotic flower) to cool and freshen the air.

Renowned Cultural Institutions

The western embankment of the Upper Lake within the new city area contains several important landmarks. The most famous of these is the Bharat Bhavan located on Shamla Hills. It is a multifaceted cultural centre of visual as well as

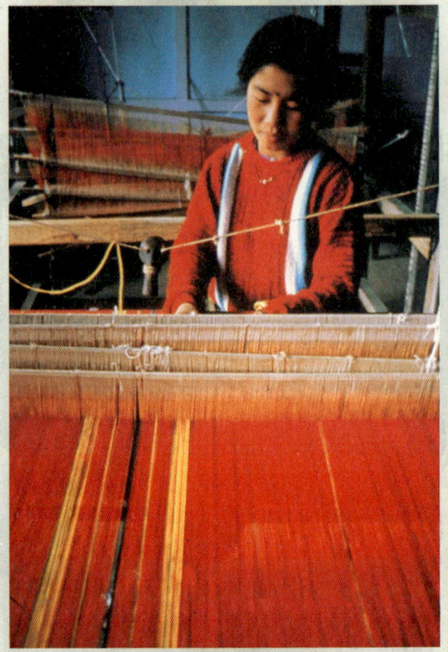

A tribal girl demostrating shawl weaving at an exhibition held at IGRMS

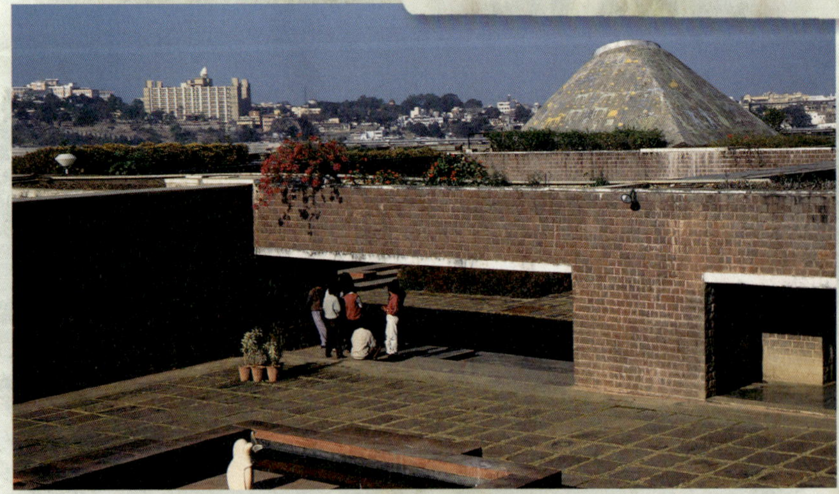

Bharat Bhavan

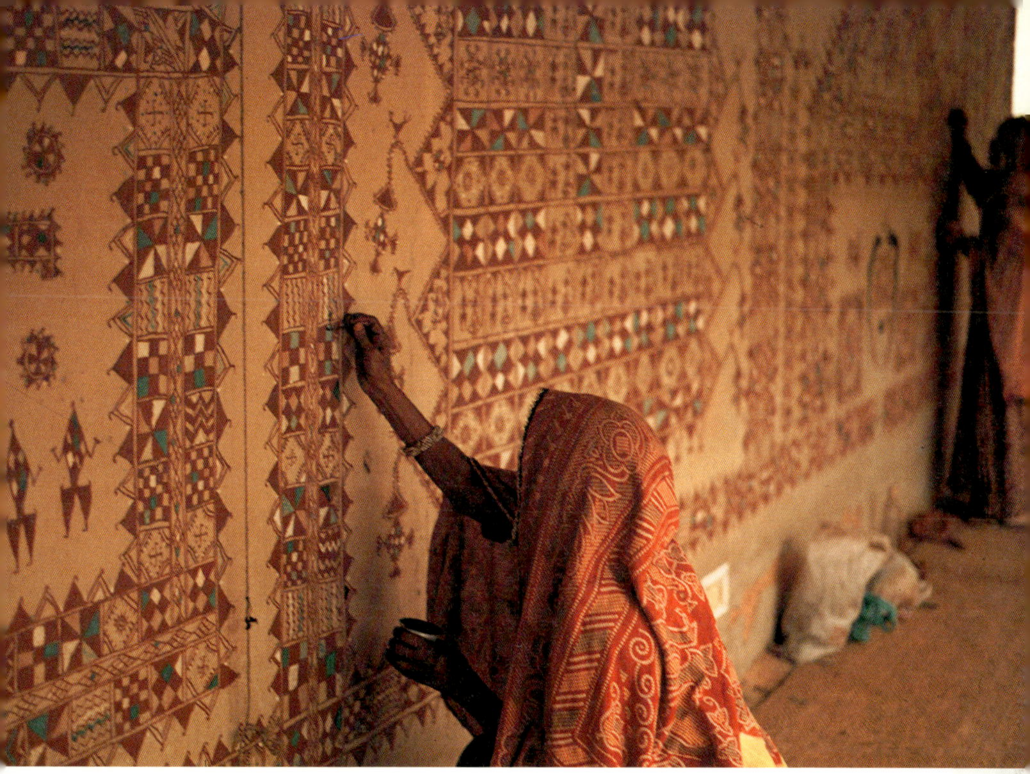

A tribal artisan at work, IGRMS (above); Tribal artisans at work, IGRMS (below)

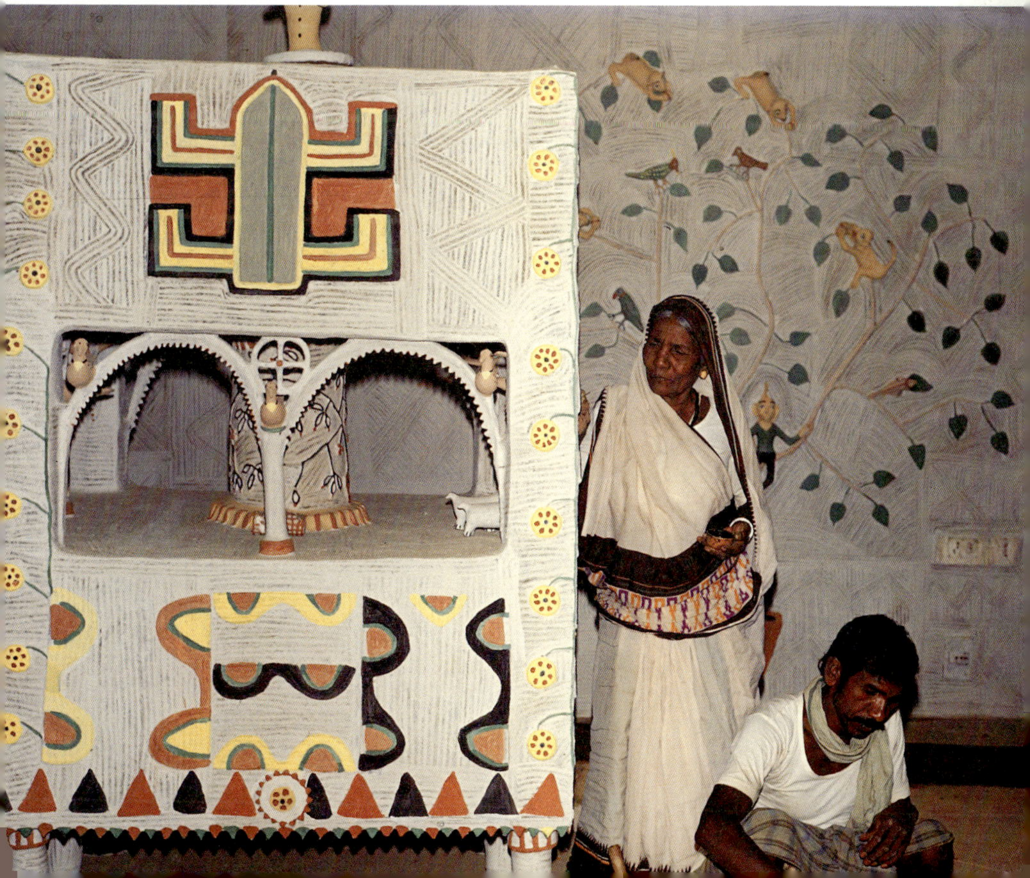

performing arts, which has no parallel in the country. Designed and created by Charles Correa, the world-famous architect, it is regarded as one of the principal centres of India for its meticulous preservation of the traditional folk art forms which have been secured in its famed gallery known as Rupankar. Other than the art gallery and museum, Bharat Bhavan also has a well-equipped big library, poetry wing and a theatre. Bhopal, regarded as one of the greatest centres for art and culture in the country, has several other cultural institutions as well, amongst these the leading one, Ravindra Bhavan, is located at the heart of the city.

Another interesting institution in this area is known as the Indira Gandhi Rashtriya Manav Sangrahalaya (IGRMS). Dedicated to the purpose of revealing the uniqueness and charm of India's land and people through the passage of time, it is an organisation

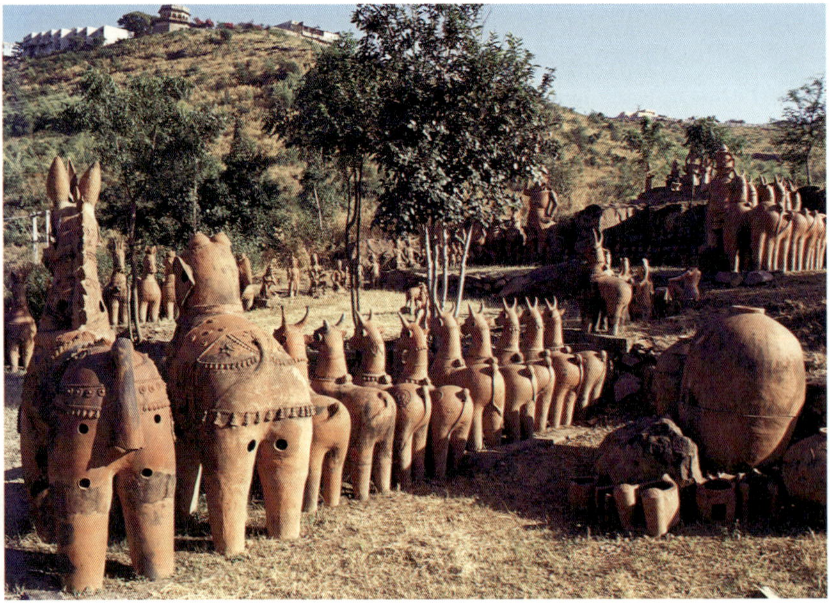

Collection of potteries from all over the country, IGRMS

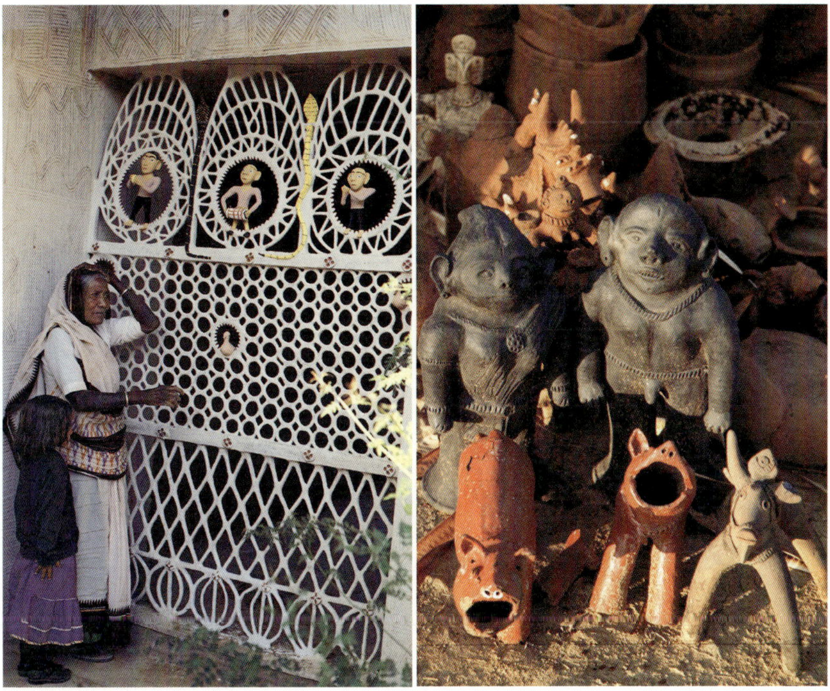

Smt Sona Bai, Rajwar President award winner, IGRMS (left); Tribal pottery displayed at IGRMS (right)

under the Ministry of Culture of the Government of India. The innovative aspects of IGRMS are its open-air as well as indoor exhibitions built with active participation of the reputed traditional artisans and experts who represent the varied communities of the Indian population. In addition, the aim is to salvage as well as to revitalise the vanishing, rare and valuable traditions of folk art and culture. Every year during the winter months, IGRMS hosts several workshops and exhibitions of rural artifacts, open-air plays, folk music and dance recitals. Tribal craftsmen and artists actively participate in large numbers to demonstrate their skills in pottery, paintings, weaving art, metal crafts as well as in the performing arts.

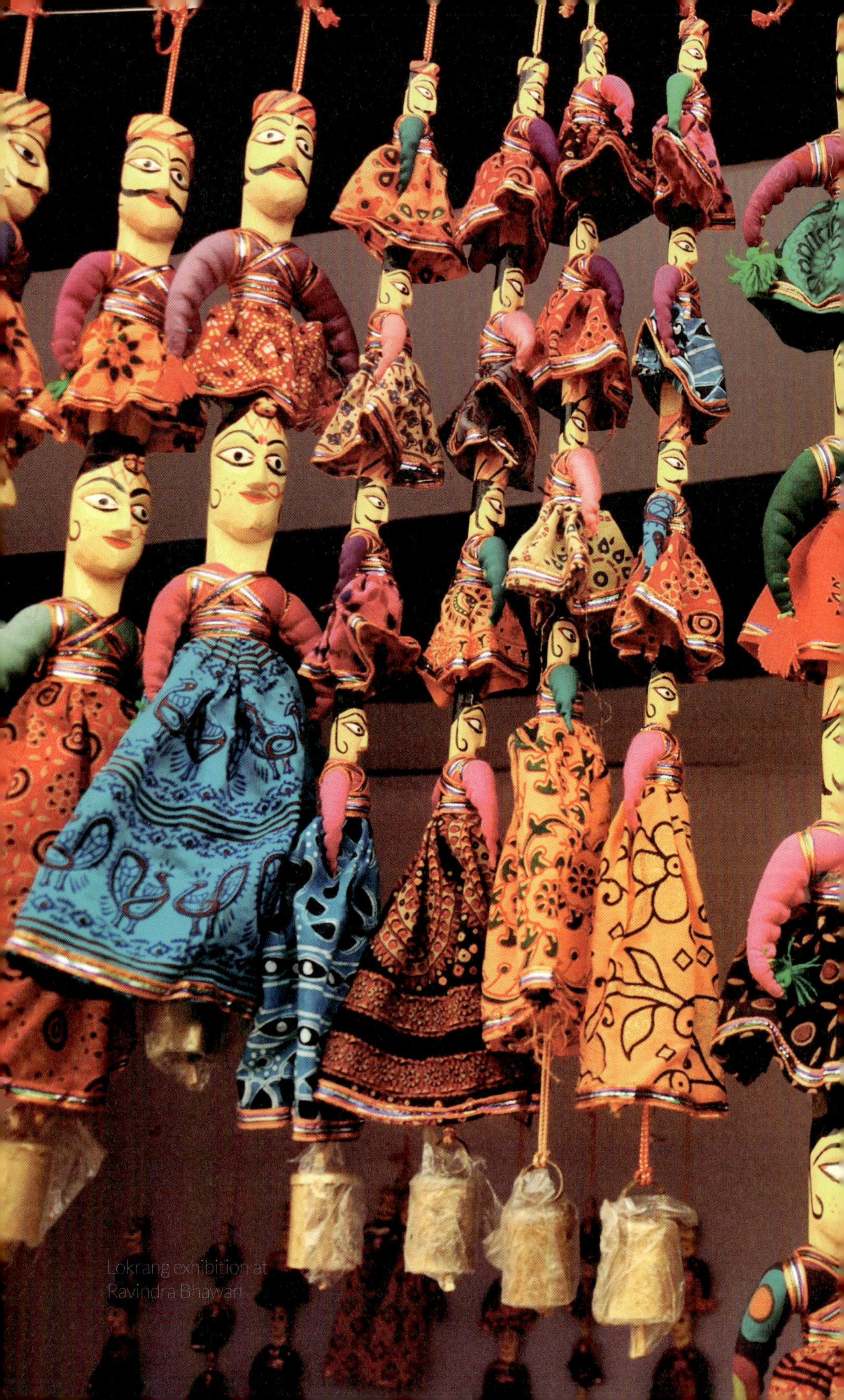

Lokrang exhibition at
Ravindra Bhawan

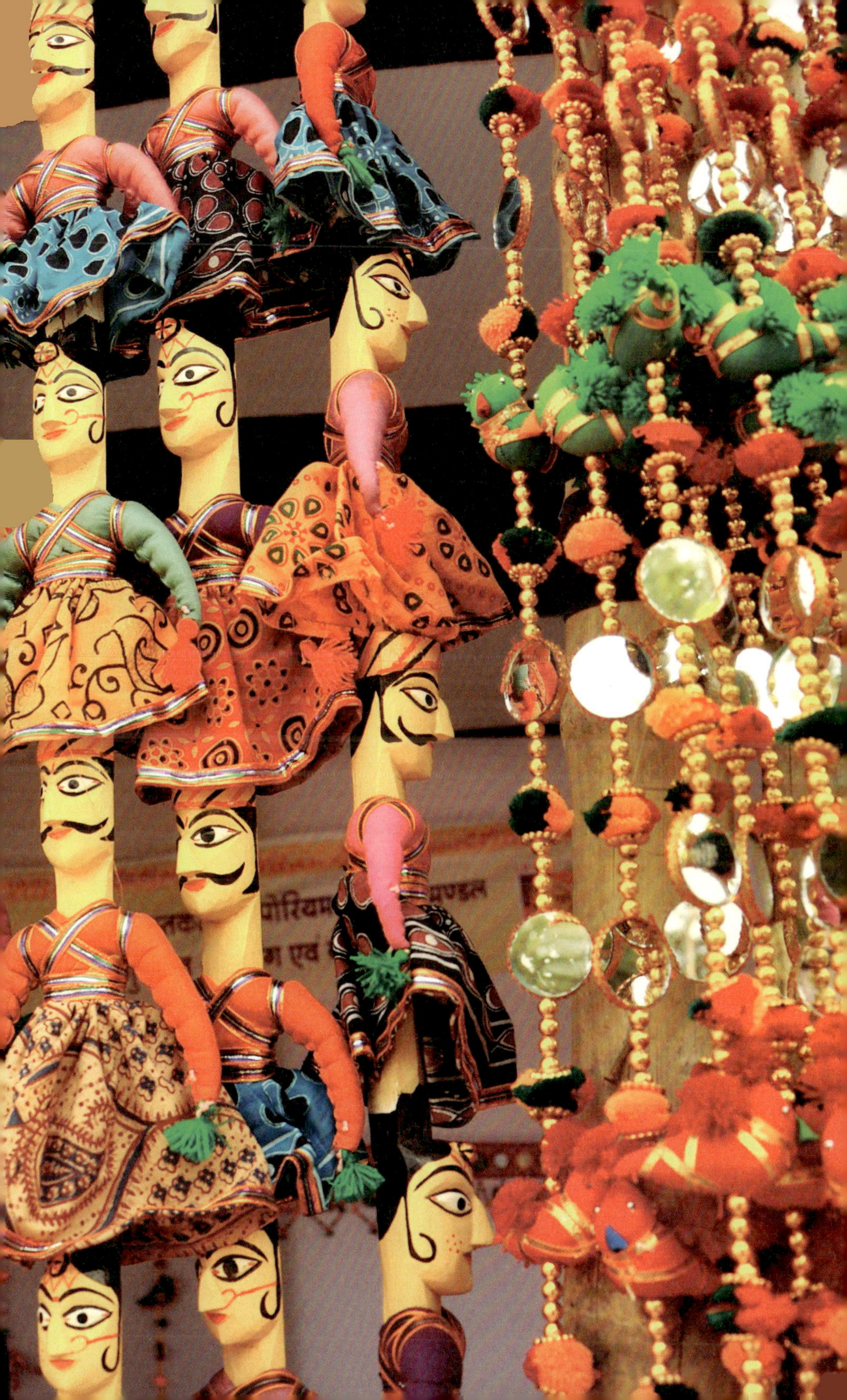

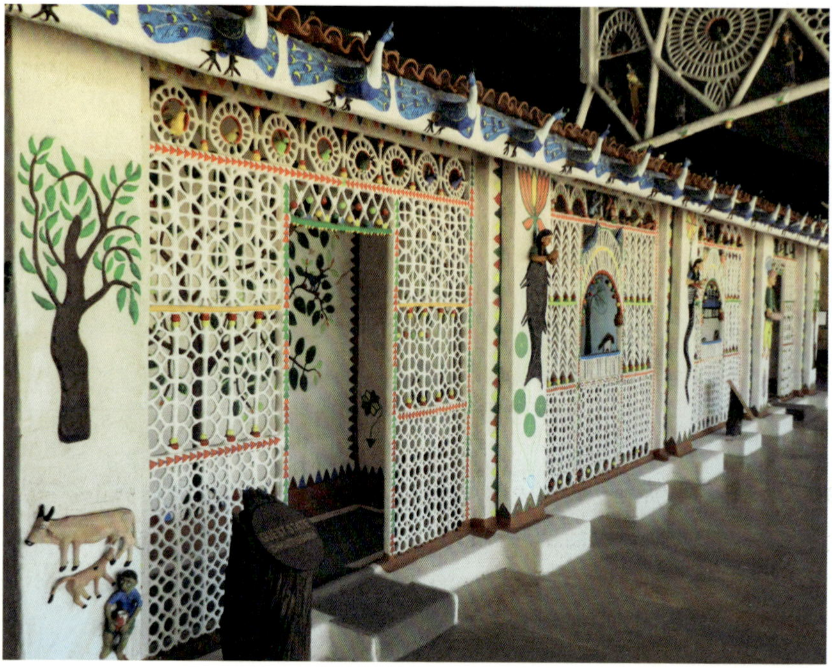

Tribal Habitat Museum (both)

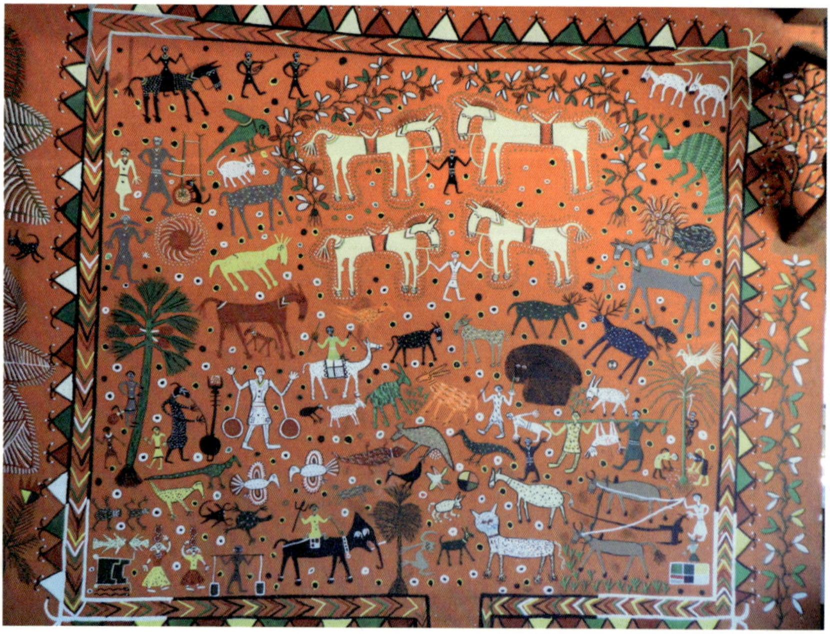

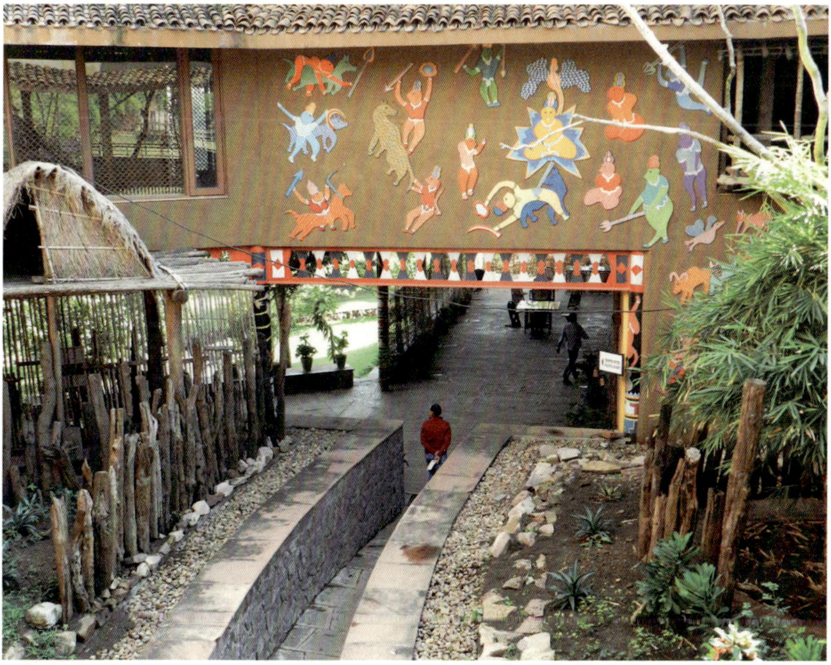

Tribal Habitat Museum (both)

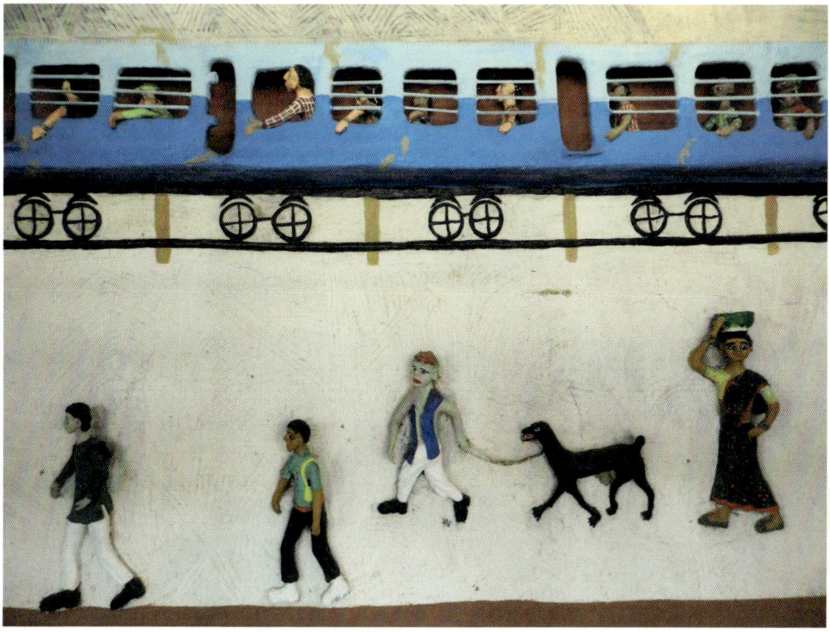

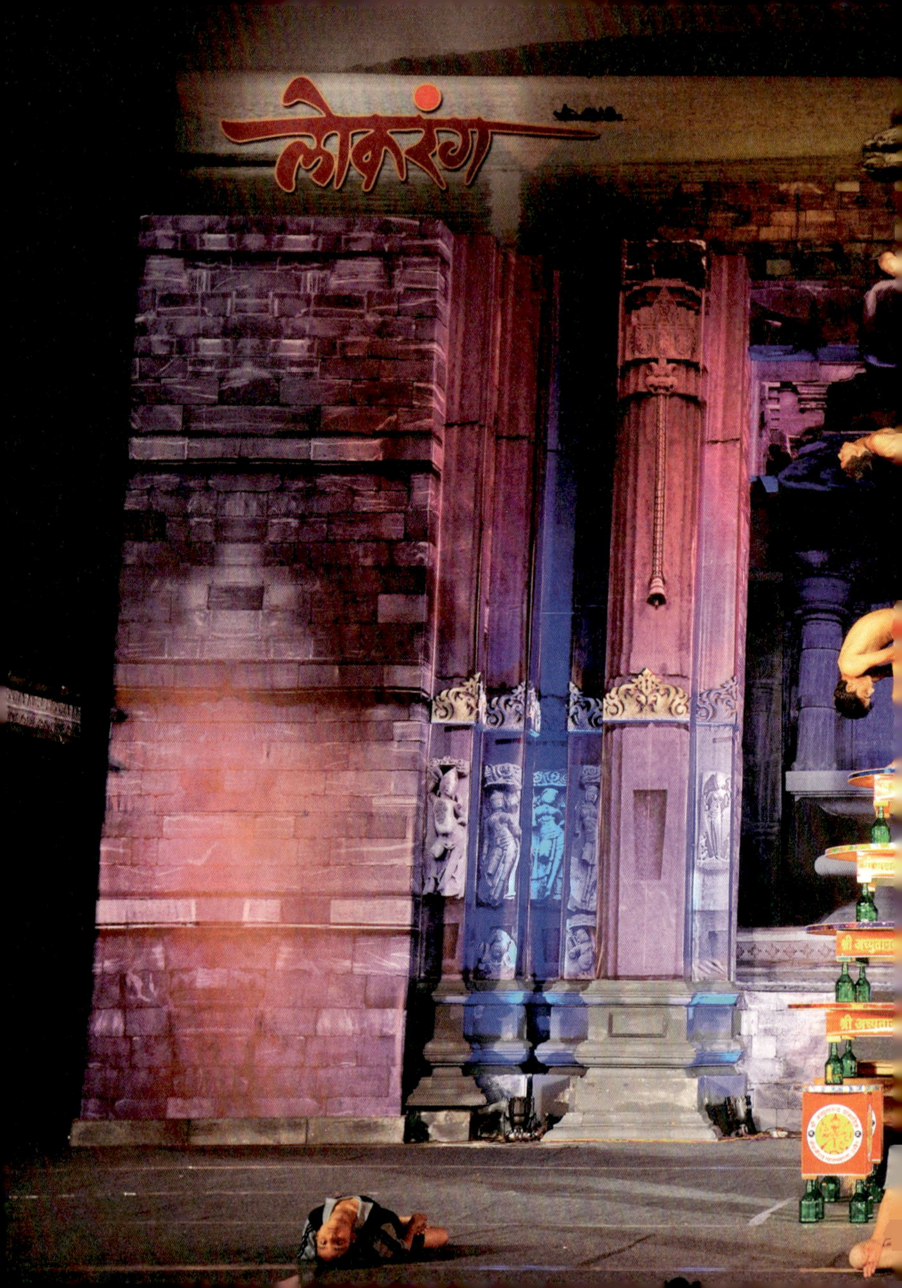
लोकरंग

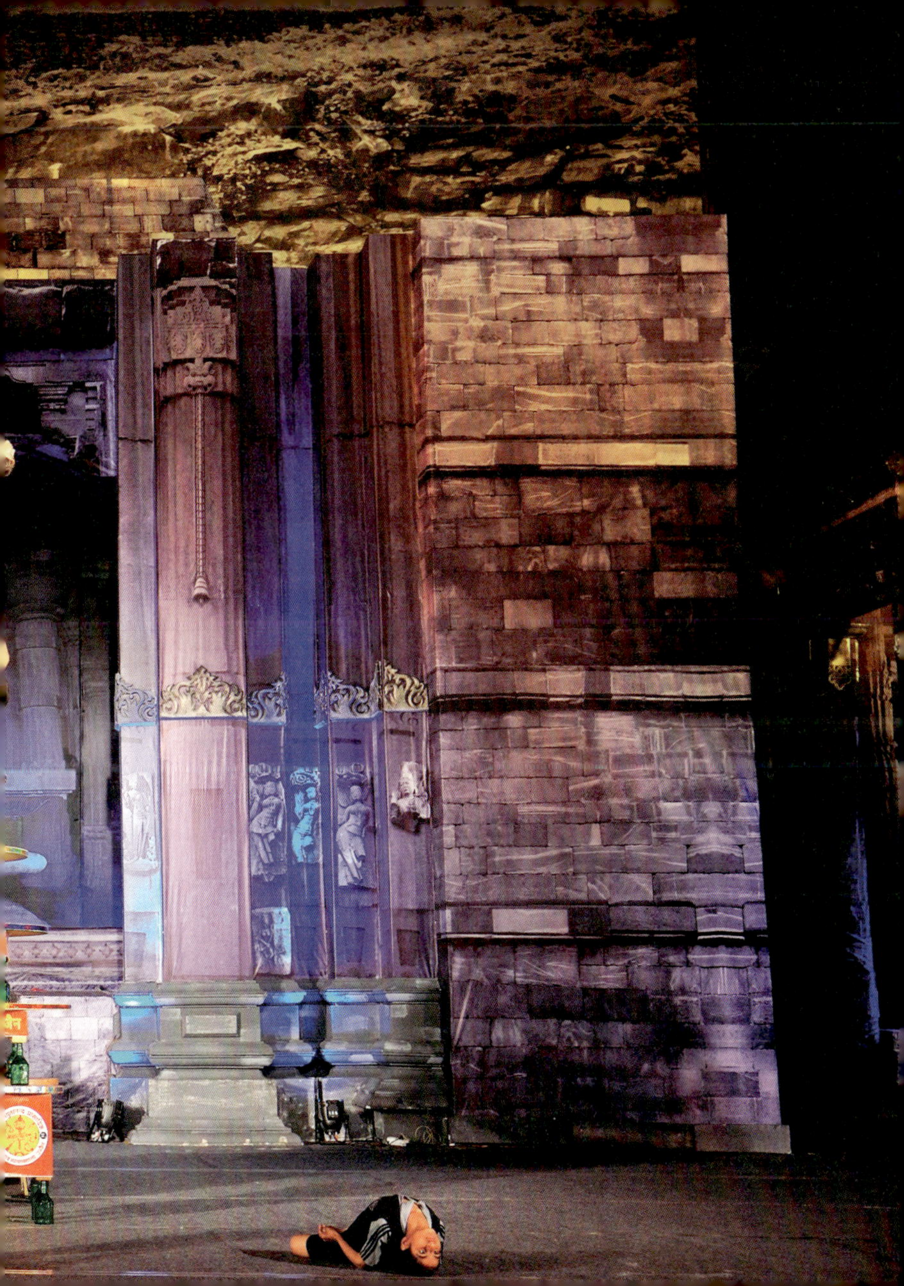

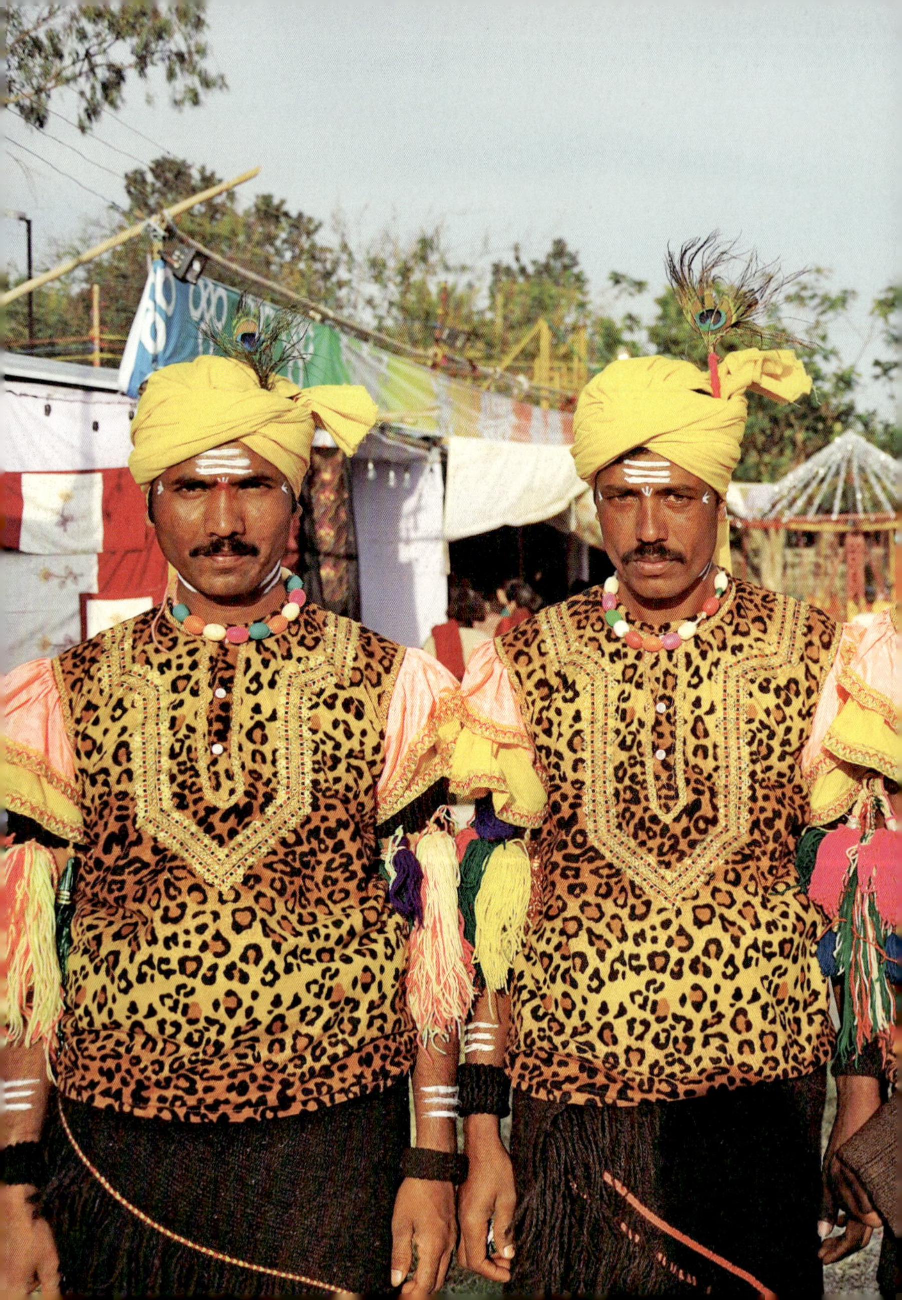

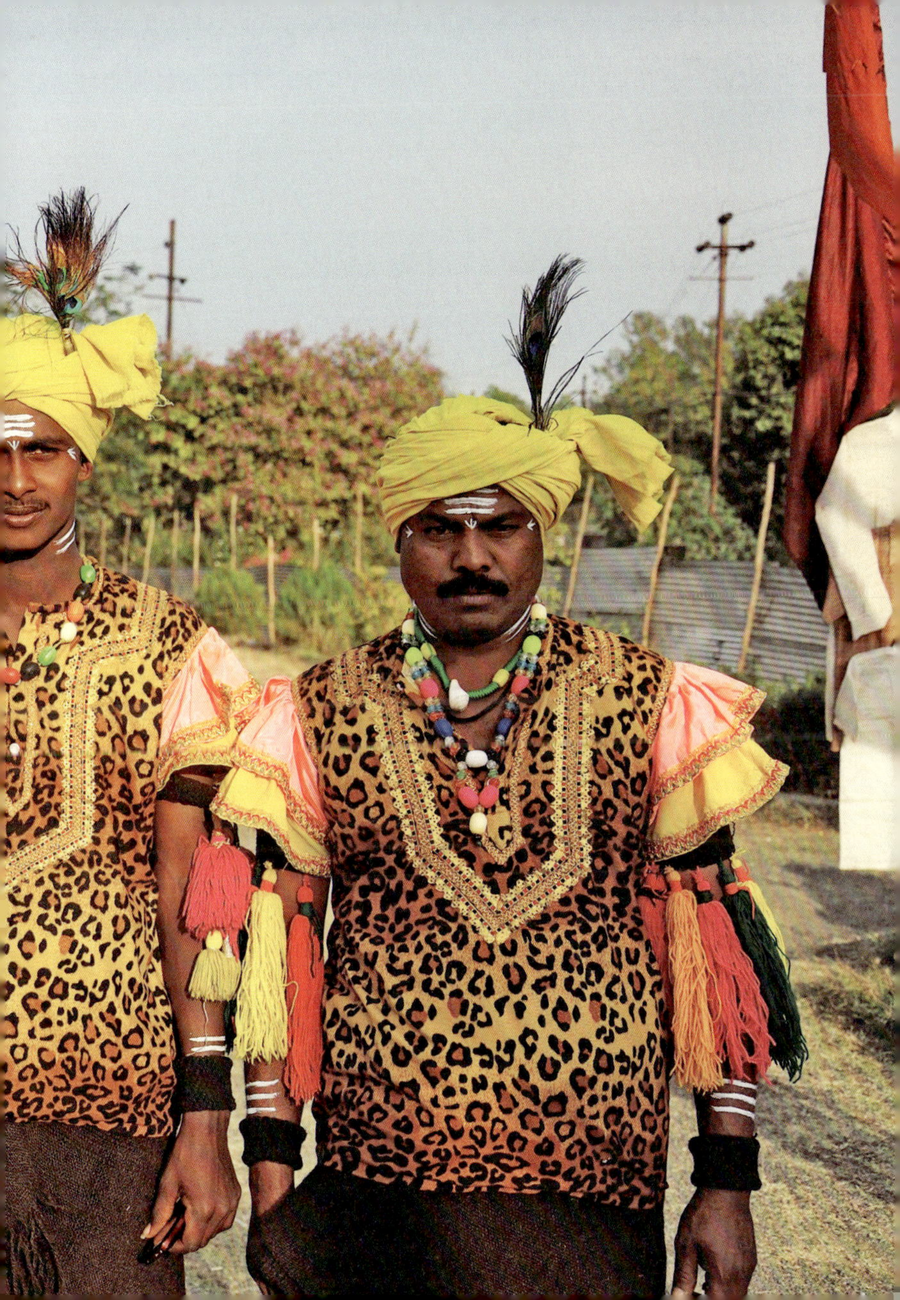

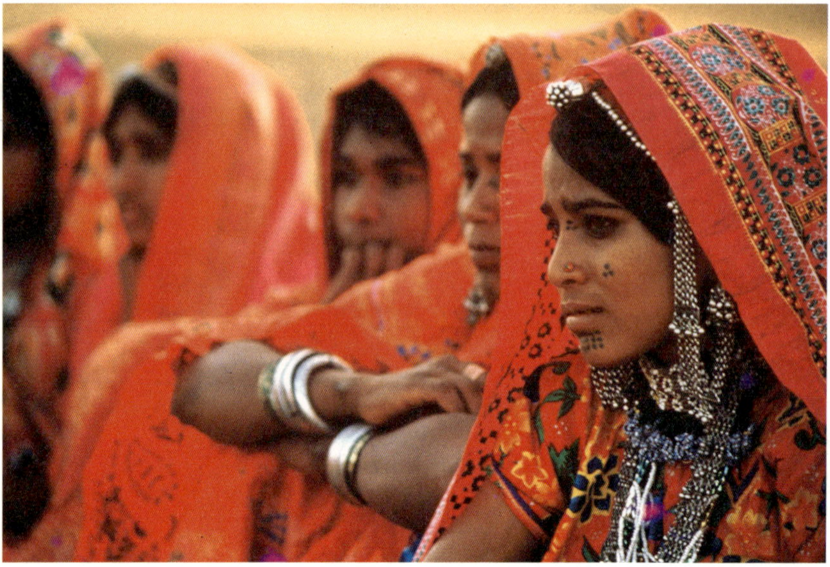

Rural women wearing traditional jewellery, Bhopal

Adjacent to IGRMS is the Tribal Museum of Madhya Pradesh State Academy established with the aim of fostering the development of tribal arts and crafts of the state. The museum displays in a big way the art, cultural traditions and the tribal artifacts of daily use; it also displays the way of life of the various tribes of the aborigines residing in the state of Madhya Pradesh including the state of Chhattisgarh, numbering the highest in the country. The purpose of this elaborate museum is to make the sophisticated modern citizens aware of the tribal people as well as care for their much needed social and economic welfare.

Photo Credits

Pgs 6-7, By Thubten Namdrol (Own work) [CC-BY-SA-3.0 (http://creativecommons.org/licenses/by-sa/3.0)], via Wikimedia Commons
Pg 19(left), [Public domain], via Wikimedia Commons
Pg 19(right), By Sir Roper Lethbridge (Golden Book of India, 1893) [Public domain], via Wikimedia Commons
Pg 30, [Public domain], via Wikimedia Commons
Pg 33, [Public domain], via Wikimedia Commons
Pg 36, By Bourne and Shepherd [Public domain], via Wikimedia Commons
Pg 38(top left), By Government of Bhopal (tonymacg on Stampsboards.com) [Public domain], via Wikimedia Commons
Pg 38(top right), By Government of Bhopal (tonymacg on Stampsboards.com) [Public domain], via Wikimedia Commons
Pg 40, By Norah Grant [Public domain], via Wikimedia Commons
Pg 41, By Wolflone (Own work) [CC-BY-SA-3.0 (http://creativecommons.org/licenses/by-sa/3.0)], via Wikimedia Commons
Pg 42, By Wolflone (Own work) [CC-BY-SA-3.0 (http://creativecommons.org/licenses/by-sa/3.0)], via Wikimedia Commons
Pg 43, By Biswarup Ganguly (Own work) [CC-BY-SA-3.0 (http://creativecommons.org/licenses/by-sa/3.0)], via Wikimedia Commons
Pg 65, By Yann (Own work) [CC BY-SA 4.0-3.0-2.5-2.0-1.0 (http://creativecommons.org/licenses/by-sa/4.0-3.0-2.5-2.0-1.0)], via Wikimedia Commons

All other photographs appearing in this book has been composed by the author.

Index